WHO WILL *SHOUT* IF NOT US?

STUDENT ACTIVISTS AND THE TIANANMEN SQUARE PROTEST, *China, 1989*

ANN **KERNS**

TfCB TWENTY-FIRST CENTURY BOOKS ■ MINNEAPOLIS

Special thanks to Gary Pranger for his knowledge and insights —AK

Twenty-First Century Books
A division of Lerner Publishing Group, Inc.
241 First Avenue North
Minneapolis, MN 55401 U.S.A.

Website address: www.lernerbooks.com

Library of Congress Cataloging-in-Publication Data

Kerns, Ann.
    Who will shout if not us? : student activists and the Tiananmen Square protest, China, 1989 / by Ann Kerns.
        p.   cm. — (Civil rights struggles around the world)
    Includes bibliographical references and index.
    ISBN 978–0–8225–8971–6 (lib. bdg. : alk. paper)
    1. Students—Political activity—China—History. 2. Student movements—China—History. 3. China—History—Tiananmen Square incident, 1989. I. Title.
LA1133.7. K47 2011
378.1'981095109048—dc22   2009049133

Manufactured in the United States of America
1 – CG – 7/15/10

CONTENTS

SPRING 1989
BEIJING, CHINA

By the late spring of 1989, China was a country in crisis. From far-flung towns to the very heart of the capital city of Beijing, the nation was wracked by protests, demonstrations, marches, sit-ins, and hunger strikes. Leading these protests were the educated youth of China—university and college students. They were supported and often joined by high school students, factory workers, farmers, office workers, and other citizens.

The protests began as a demand for government reform. The students claimed that the government's only political party, the Chinese Communist Party (CCP), ignored corruption in its own ranks. It failed to listen to its citizens' legitimate and legal complaints. As the weeks went on, the student protest movement grew and strengthened.

A demonstrator speaks to the growing crowd in Tiananmen Square in Beijing, China, in the late spring of 1989.

The Chinese government was shocked by the extent of the movement. As large as China is, the government was used to having an enormous measure of control over citizens. Communist Party leaders watched the protests with great concern from inside Zhongnanhai, the government center in Beijing. They watched them figuratively and literally, for the protest movement was taking place close to Zhongnanhai, in Beijing's Tiananmen Square.

Beginning in April and throughout May 1989, tens of thousands of protesters and their supporters gathered in the public square each day. The students demanded that high-ranking government officials come out and meet with them. But the few attempts that the government and students made at dialogue quickly broke down. Each side dug into its position. The students began to organize themselves, publicize their demands, and reach out to national and international supporters. Meanwhile, Chinese leaders argued behind closed doors about the best way to end the protests.

Soon the students came to believe that the government had no intention of listening to their demands. The government became convinced that something much larger and more dangerous than student politics was behind the protest movement. It saw the hand of the party's political enemies working to bring down the government. The standoff continued, and splits appeared among the protesters and the government leaders. Hard-liners on both sides gained power.

By late May, the government decided that the only solution was a drastic one. It mobilized the army to end the protests and clear Tiananmen Square. But many students and citizens refused to let the soldiers and tanks into Beijing without a fight. The result was death, injury, and near chaos in the city. The conflict sent student leaders to prison or into exile and caused the fall of some key government officials.

The international community watched in shock as the events at Tiananmen Square unfolded. In TV broadcasts and publications around the world, people everywhere witnessed the Chinese government using soldiers, tanks, and military weapons to crush a protest led by unarmed citizens. Many people in the United States and Europe saw a simple conflict: young protesters demanding Western-style democracy

Crowds prevent soldiers from moving toward Tiananmen Square on June 2, 1989. A few days later, tanks rolled into the square.

and freedom from a repressive Communist government. Tiananmen Square was added to the long list of the world's civil rights struggles. But how did the confrontation in Beijing go so wrong?

Understanding the spring 1989 events and aftermath is a difficult task. The Chinese government has clearly said that it feels no obligation to explain its decisions to the outside world. It has released few documents and statements concerning the events. It has rejected facts, figures, eyewitness accounts, and human rights complaints generated by Western news media and other organizations. Much of what is known and has been published in the West comes from Western observers

and Chinese students who fled the country. The Chinese government dismisses many important details in those versions of events as anti-Communist propaganda.

To approach the topic, readers must understand how the Chinese Communist Party operates and what internal leadership tensions were brought into play that spring. It is also crucial to understand what the students were demanding of party leaders and what fueled the escalating protests. Tiananmen Square 1989 has its roots in history and was shaped by China's unique culture. Its effects continue to be felt in China and beyond.

CHAPTER 1

CHINA
IN THE
TWENTIETH
CENTURY

Not to have a correct political point
of view is like having no soul."

–Chinese leader Mao Zedong, on the importance
of studying political ideology, 1957

Archaeologists have found evidence of human settlement in China dating back to 5000 B.C. Those ancient findings include elements that have echoed throughout centuries of Chinese culture—for example, dragon designs on pottery and jade carvings. Such evidence indicates that China is one of the oldest continuous civilizations in the world.

China is also the world's largest and most populous nation. For many centuries, the vast territories of China were ruled by a succession of dynasties. In a dynasty, ruling power is passed down through or inherited by family members. At the head of each Chinese dynasty was an emperor—the supreme ruler believed to be chosen by heaven to unite the people.

For most of its history, China was an agrarian society. Agrarian refers to farming. Most Chinese people lived on small farms or in rural villages. The imperial courts—the centers of power—were located in China's larger cities. Since the early fifteenth century A.D., Chinese emperors have ruled from Beijing.

With the emperor as the strong central authority, the empire's day-to-day business was administered by a vast bureaucracy, or network of government officials. Village and town leaders presided over legal disputes and collected taxes. These leaders reported to bureaucratic officials, and those officials sent reports back to Beijing.

Dragons appear in Chinese art and architecture throughout its history. This dragon is part of a Nine Dragon Screen in Beihai Park in Beijing.

■ REVOLUTION

In the early twentieth century, the rule of the emperors ended. Rebellion grew out of frustration with government corruption and foreign interference. In 1912 rebels forced the last emperor, Pu Yi, out of power during the Xinhai Revolution. The revolutionaries, led by Sun Yat-sen (Sun Zhongzhan), wanted to establish a republic (a form of government with elected leaders). Sun founded a new political party, the Kuomintang (Nationalist Party, or KMT).

Sun's leadership was challenged by Yuan Shikai, a powerful warlord from northern China. In 1913 Yuan forced Sun into exile in Japan. Three years later, Yuan died. Sun returned to China and regained control of the southern provinces. But the north descended into a war among competing warlords and their armies.

As China struggled for stability, an international crisis intervened: World War I (1914–1918). At the end of the war, Germany signed a peace treaty with the Allies (France, Great Britain, Japan, the United States, and other nations). Called the Treaty of Versailles, it was signed in 1919. But the treaty was not good news for China.

Top: **Pu Yi was the last emperor of China.** *Bottom:* **Sun Yat-sen was the first president of the Chinese Republic.**

The treaty's terms gave important Chinese territories to Japan. These territories had been taken from China by Japan during the war. This action greatly angered many Chinese. On May 4, 1919, more than three thousand Beijing university students began a series of protests. The May Fourth Movement came to symbolize China's sense of nationhood and patriotism. It also symbolized China's often unhappy relations with powerful Western countries.

In 1921 another Chinese political party formed, the Chinese Communist Party. The CCP was founded on the principles of Communism, a political theory in which social and economic classes are abolished and all people are regarded as equals. The KMT also admitted Communist members. But most of the KMT's leaders were urban intellectuals (people who make their living writing, teaching, studying, or researching) and wealthy landowners. Although the two parties had little in common, they fought together against the northern warlords.

Sun Yat-sen died in 1925, and Chiang Kai-shek took control of the KMT. The allied parties defeated the warlords in 1927 but quickly turned on each other. When the Communists tried to grab power, Chiang responded with a brutal suppression. About five thousand people were killed. Chiang also began purging, or driving out, Communists from the KMT. He established the KMT as the ruling party of China.

Chiang Kai-shek (right) poses with Chinese leader Chang Hsueh-liang in the 1930s.

In the latter half of the nineteenth century, much of Europe and the United States underwent an enormous change called the Industrial Revolution. Before that time, most people lived on farms or in small rural towns. Most goods—food, clothing, and tools, for example— were produced locally and sold in small markets. The Industrial Revolution replaced those small local operations with large factories owned by capitalists (wealthy investors). The Industrial Revolution was encouraged by a free-market economy (an economy with few government restrictions). Many people left their farms and rural towns to move to large cities to work in the factories and try to earn their share in a booming economy.

The Industrial Revolution produced many advances in technology and made a wide variety of goods available to more people. It also created a large middle class—merchants, highly skilled workers, and educated professionals (such as engineers and bankers). But to some observers, industrialization created a very serious social problem—the exploitation of lower-class workers. Factories wanted to produce the most goods in the cheapest and quickest manner. There were few rules governing workers' rights, fair pay, reasonable working hours, and safe conditions.

In response to this exploitation, some social critics and political philosophers, such as Karl Marx (1818–1883) (right), began to argue against capitalism and a free-market economy. They argued that governments should have more control over industry and the marketplace. Some believed that governments should take over the economy on behalf of the workers, as a first step toward an egalitarian (based on equality), classless society. Variations of this philosophy were called Socialism and Communism.

Socialism and Communism became a major political force in the twentieth century. While in exile in Europe, V. I. Lenin (1870–1924) became the leader of the Russian Communists. Lenin believed workers were the engine of revolution. In 1917 Lenin's Communist Party overthrew the Russian government, and in 1922, Russia became the Union of Soviet Socialist Republics (USSR, or the Soviet Union). Marxist and Leninist philosophy became the basis for modern Communism. And the Soviet Union became a model for the Socialist and Communist states that followed in China, Eastern Europe, Southeast Asia, and Cuba.

In theory, Communist governments operate for the benefit of working-class people. They emphasize equality and the power of the people. But in practice, most Communist countries are one-party states. Leaders are chosen by the party, not elected by the people. Historically, people in Communist countries have had little to say about how the government operates. And they have little control over their lives. They are told where to work and where to live. Communist governments have relied on spying, intimidation, imprisonment, and violence to control their populations and avoid "counterrevolutions" (the overthrow of the revolutionary Communist government by discontented citizens).

The KMT and the CCP had to join forces again in 1937, as China went to war against Japan. World War II (1939–1945) began soon after, and China found itself on the side of the Western Allies against Japan, Germany, and other Axis powers. During the war, the CCP moved farther into the countryside, where it established bases and attracted many followers. It developed a military force called the Red Army.

By the end of World War II, China was almost bankrupt and the KMT was weakened. The two parties refused to work together, and in 1946, civil war broke out between the Communists and the Nationalists. By the autumn of 1949, the Communists' Red Army had taken over most of China. On October 1, Communist leader Mao Zedong declared victory. In Beijing's Tiananmen Square, he announced the establishment of the People's Republic of China (PRC). The Red Army became the People's Liberation Army (PLA)—the defenders and protectors of Chinese citizens. Chiang and the KMT fled to Taiwan, an island off the southeastern coast of China.

MODERN CHINA

CHAIRMAN MAO

Mao established the Chinese Communist Party as the People's Republic's only political party. He became the chairman of the CCP. His close CCP comrade, Zhou Enlai, became the first premier (leader) of the PRC. Mao and Zhou undertook to transform China through a Communist revolution.

Mao believed that Communism could defeat the foreign interference and internal corruption that had plagued China. Communism would create a classless, egalitarian China. It would adopt democratic principles, so that the people would have a direct say in how the country was governed. Eventually, there would be no need for a government or state. The country would be ruled by the people. But

Mao Zedong declares victory over the Chinese nationalists in Tiananmen Square on October 1, 1949.

true Communism could not take place immediately. First, China needed a period of transition called Socialism, during which the state protected the people's interests and provided national security.

COMRADES

In Communist China, government officials and party members address one another as "comrade." The term means "fellow soldier," a reference to party members' experience as revolutionaries. By the late 1980s, *comrade* was used mostly by older party members.

The redistribution of land was one part of Mao's reform. Mao's government took rural land from wealthy landowners and began giving it to poor peasants. Another step was for the government to take control of the economy. In a Communist state, the government controls the means of production and distribution of goods. The government decides how factories are run, how much the factories are expected to produce, and how those products are sold. It decides where people will work and how much they will be paid by assigning employment. It even takes control of where workers live by assigning housing. The Communist state has a huge impact on people's daily lives.

In the manufacturing part of the economy, Mao focused on heavy industry, such as steel production. In the agricultural sector, he organized small family farms into large cooperatives, or communes. Farmers sold their harvests to the government, which paid them a set price for food. For the first few years, the economy did well. But by 1956, it was clear that the farming communes were much less successful than industrial factories.

■ THE GREAT LEAP FORWARD

To help solve this issue, Mao called on China's intellectuals to offer suggestions and criticisms. All those varying views, Mao declared, would be like the blossoming of a hundred flowers. But the Hundred Flowers Campaign did not last. The suggestions and criticisms were more numerous and more severe than Mao expected. Feeling that his leadership was threatened, Mao ended the campaign in 1957. He forced outspoken intellectuals from their jobs or had them imprisoned.

Mao developed his own radical solution to the country's economic problems. He called his plan the Great Leap Forward. The plan put more than 100 million people to work on projects involving physical labor. Workers were sent to the countryside to dig irrigation ditches, create farm fields on unused land, and operate small-scale steel furnaces. Mao's plan was to make China completely self-sufficient so that it would not have to buy food or products from Western countries.

Like the Chinese emperors, Mao relied on a vast bureaucracy to run his Communist nation. Party members and officials around the

Workers build steel smelting furnaces in Beijing in 1958 during the Great Leap Forward.

country reported to Beijing. Officials also set up production schedules and targets—how much each farm or factory was expected to produce by a certain date. But the schedules and targets only worked on paper. In reality, crops on the communal farms began going to waste because workers had no efficient way to store or transport them. Farming practices on the communes resulted in severe damage to the soil. Agricultural production fell, and food shortages began. The food shortages turned into famine, and more than twenty million people starved to death between 1958 and 1962.

The Chinese Communist Party is not an official governing body. But in China's one-party state, it holds supreme political power. CCP members dominate the ranks of the National People's Congress (*below, voting in 1981*). It is the highest body of state power, according to the PRC's constitution.

The CCP is organized around its own National Congress, its highest body, according to the party's constitution. The party's congress meets once every five years. One of the functions of the congress is to elect a Central Committee, which has about three hundred members. When the congress is not in session, the Central Committee is authorized to make decisions for the party.

Within the Central Committee is the Politburo, which has between nineteen and twenty-five members. Officially, the Central Committee chooses Politburo members. But in practice, the Politburo appoints its own new members.

Power within the Politburo is concentrated in the Politburo Standing Committee. The Standing Committee consists of between five and nine members. These members are the most powerful people in the CCP and, thus, the most powerful people in government.

THE CULTURAL REVOLUTION

CCP leadership tried to fix the problems in the Great Leap plan. Communist leaders such as Deng Xiaoping urged Mao to take more moderate Socialist steps toward Communism. Mao reasserted his authority and held to his plan, until it became clear that the situation could not go on. In an emergency measure, China bought grain from Western countries and broke up the farming communes into small family farms.

Mao agreed to these solutions. But he began to suspect that some party leaders were using the opportunity to introduce Western capitalist practices. Doing so, Mao said, would derail China's path toward true Communism. It would bring back government corruption and the huge gap between the wealthy and the poor. Feeling that his leadership and Socialist vision were under attack, Mao struck back.

Early in 1966, Mao began the Cultural Revolution to set China back on what he believed to be the correct path to Communism. He removed Deng Xiaoping and other moderates from office. Deng was placed under house arrest, meaning that he could not leave his home.

Mao's wife, Jiang Qing, joined with three close associates, Zhang Chunqiao, Yao Wenyuan, and Wang Hongwen. They became known as the Gang of Four. The gang took a fanatical approach to the battles of the Cultural Revolution. They denounced any intellectuals, artists, or government officials who disagreed with Mao's theories and policies.

In June 1966, Mao called on all Chinese people to denounce bourgeois values. The bourgeoisie, or middle class, Mao claimed, would always act in their own interest to secure wealth and power. Their values—such as accumulating personal wealth, raising their social status, and owning property—made the bourgeoisie the enemy of the Socialist state.

Young people responded most readily to Mao's cultural war. High school and university students across the country formed groups called the Red Guards. Mao and the Gang of Four encouraged the students, and the ranks of the Red Guards swelled. In August 1966, China's schools and universities closed, and millions of students devoted themselves full-time to the revolution.

Mao Zedong was the most influential figure in twentieth-century China. His commitment to Communism shaped modern Chinese politics and gave the country a sense of nationhood. His errors caused misery, fear, and death for millions of people.

Mao was born in 1893 in Shaoshan, a rural community in Hunan Province in southeastern China. His parents were well-to-do peasants, and Mao was educated in traditional Chinese subjects. After secondary school, he moved to Hunan's capital, Changsha, to study at the Hunan Teachers College. While there, he fought in the Xinhai Revolution to overthrow the emperor. He finished his degree and, in 1918, became a librarian at Beijing University. There he began studying Marxist political theory, rejecting traditional Chinese values.

Mao was present at the founding of the Chinese Communist Party in 1921. He became active in the party and began writing articles and papers. But Mao's political theories began to deviate from the CCP's strict Marxism. He believed that a Communist revolution must be led by the mass of peasant farmers, not by a small, educated group.

In 1925 Mao returned to Shaoshan to organize peasants into labor unions. After Chiang Kai-shek began purging Communists from the KMT in the late 1920s, Mao also organized the peasants into fighting forces. He gained power in the CCP. Over the next eighteen years, through World War II, Mao organized peasant unions and built the Red Army into a large, disciplined force. Immediately after the war, he established the People's Republic of China and drove the KMT out of mainland China.

As chairman of the CCP, Mao set about making China into a Socialist society. He based his plans on the idea of a peasant revolution, in which society would be upended. Wealth would be redistributed, and social classes would be eliminated. But Mao's policies during the Great Leap Forward failed. In reaction to criticism and alternative theories within the CCP, Mao became increasingly autocratic. He demanded and rewarded loyalty. During the Cultural Revolution, his followers raised Mao to an almost godlike figure.

After Mao's death in 1976, Deng Xiaoping issued the official CCP view of Mao's legacy. Mao was judged to have made some errors but was acknowledged as a great leader. His preserved body still lies in a glass coffin in a memorial hall on Tiananmen Square. A huge portrait of him hangs over Tiananmen, the gate to the Forbidden City (below), the former palace of the Chinese emperor.

The Red Guards criticized their teachers and university administrators as being elitist and bourgeois. On Mao's orders, the Red Guards tried to do away with anything that belonged to the pre-Communist way of life, which they labeled "old China." Books and artwork were burned. Temples, shrines, and museums were ransacked and destroyed. Artists and intellectuals were dragged into so-called struggle sessions, in which they were beaten and humiliated by Red Guards. Thousands were executed, died from physical abuse, or

Red Guards march through Beijing in 1966. Many of the Red Guards were former students responding to Mao's call to reject bourgeois (middle-class) values.

The color red is strongly associated with Communism. To Communists, red symbolizes revolution. During the Cultural Revolution, Red Guards wore red armbands or red scarves and had red stars on their caps. They carried a collection of Mao's quotations called *The Little Red Book*.

committed suicide out of fear. Those who survived were thrown in prison or sent to the countryside to do hard labor.

By 1976 fighting had broken out among rival Red Guard factions. Mao was forced to send in the army to try to restore order. He sent many young people into the country to work on farms. He reopened schools, and students were ordered to attend (although they only studied Mao's teachings). The most radical elements of the Red Guards faded away.

Mao died in September 1976. Hua Guofeng became the new chairman of the CCP. The Gang of Four planned to stage a coup (overthrow of government) to seize power. But Hua learned of the plot. His guards surrounded and arrested the gang. The Cultural Revolution was over.

DENG XIAOPING

Hua welcomed Deng and other moderates back into the party in 1977. Deng returned as a member of the Politburo, the central policymaking group within the CCP. But Deng soon began criticizing Hua. The previous decades had left China weak, impoverished, and isolated from the rest of the world. The Cultural Revolution had all but destroyed the Communist Party. People no longer trusted it. Deng believed that Hua was not moving fast enough to fix these problems. More decisive reforms were needed to restore China and the CCP. In 1978 Deng forced Hua from office and took over as the head of the CCP.

Deng's plan for reform involved the Four Modernizations. These modernizations would put China on equal footing with the rest of the world in four areas: agriculture, industry, defense, and technology. He put an end to farming communes and introduced some free-market measures by allowing farmers to sell their own products. Deng also encouraged the growth of private businesses and allowed foreigners to invest in regions called special economic zones. He ordered the building of modern factories and bought modern weapons for the military.

The government still controlled newspapers and radio and television stations. The national daily newspaper, the *People's Daily*, was run by CCP members. So was China Central Television (CCTV), the national TV network. Xinhua News Agency (an organization that collects and sends news stories to other publications) was run by the government. Still, Deng allowed reporters, artists, and writers more freedom than they'd had in previous decades.

Deng also restored the prestige of the universities. The number of students and college teachers grew, and many new universities opened to accommodate them. To help China modernize, Deng sent students to study science and technology in other countries. And to end China's isolation, Deng himself traveled abroad to forge diplomatic ties and trade relations.

> **"It doesn't matter whether a cat is black or white, as long as it catches mice."**
>
> —Deng Xiaoping's motto regarding his use of capitalist elements in economic reform, n.d.

Deng also began reforms within the Communist Party. The Great Leap Forward and the Cultural Revolution had been disasters for China. But Mao was still a powerful and, in many cases, an admired figure. Deng carefully praised Mao's early achievements and criticized his later

Students study in the library of Qinghua University in Beijing in 1985, after Deng's reforms restored the prestige of higher education in China.

mistakes. Then, to move the party past the Mao era, Deng pushed older party officials into retirement and recruited younger party members. He gave positions of power to more reform-minded CCP members, such as Zhao Ziyang and Hu Yaobang.

Deng encouraged the suggestions of younger people and intellectuals in general. In late 1978, he set up a Democracy Wall in Beijing. This long brick wall on Xidan Street provided a public place for citizens to post art and essays expressing their opinions on government. But like Mao during the Hundred Flowers Campaign, Deng got a fiercer response than he bargained for.

Wei Jingsheng, an electrician and former PLA soldier, used the wall to call for a "fifth modernization": democracy. Wei did not believe that Deng's plans would truly help China. "We want a modern lifestyle and democracy for the people," Wei declared. "Freedom and happiness are our sole objectives in accomplishing modernization. Without this fifth modernization all others are merely another promise."

In a democracy, Wei wrote, the people choose their government representatives in free elections. Wei argued that this is the only power the mass of people have to fight oppression and exploitation. It formed the basis for any individual's "pursuit of happiness and prosperity." Other writers agreed, calling on the government to ensure basic freedoms and human rights. Unless these were guaranteed, activists said, China had no future in the modern world.

Deng saw this activism as a personal attack on him and a challenge to the CCP's one-party rule. The wall was closed in 1979, and Wei and several others were arrested for counterrevolutionary (working against the Communist revolution) activities.

DEMOCRACY

The Chinese word for democracy is minzhu. Min means "the people." Zhu means "to be in charge." Democracy is not a Western or contrary concept in Chinese Communism. In theory, Communism expresses the will of the people, and democracy is the means by which the people make known that will. But student demonstrators calling for democracy in the 1980s seemed to mean different things. Some meant that the government should reform and return to its Communist roots. But others were clearly rejecting Communism and equating democracy with a Western-style government.

Wei Jingsheng testifies during his trial in Beijing in 1979. He was tried and convicted of counterrevolutionary activities as part of Deng's crackdown.

REFORM AND CORRUPTION

In 1980 Deng's protégé Zhao Ziyang became premier of the People's Republic of China. In 1981 another Deng follower, Hu Yaobang, became general secretary of the Communist Party. As such, Hu was the party's highest official. Like Deng, Zhao and Hu believed in free-market reforms for China. At this stage in the Socialist transformation, they declared, China could use capitalist tactics (such as a free market) to encourage economic growth and power.

Deng Xiaoping came to wield enormous political power in China in the 1970s. He straddled two eras in Chinese history—an insular (inward-looking), revolutionary China and a modern China looking to compete in a global economy.

Deng was born in 1904 in Sichuan, a province in central China. His family belonged to the landlord class, and Deng received a good education. As a teenager, he traveled to France and Moscow (the capital of the USSR), where he became interested in Communist politics. He joined the Communist Party in 1924.

Deng returned to China in 1927 and went to work for the CCP. When China went to war with Japan in 1937, Deng became a political official with the 129th division of the Chinese army. That division grew, and Deng rose through the ranks of the party.

In 1954 Deng became the party's secretary-general. He also became a member of the Politburo. In 1956 he was appointed general secretary of the Politburo Standing Committee. As Deng became more powerful, he pushed for his vision of economic reform. In the 1960s, during the Cultural Revolution, he was accused of being a capitalist. He was purged (expelled) from the party and placed under house arrest. With the help of Zhou Enlai, Deng returned to power within the party in 1973. He was purged again briefly in 1976 by the Gang of Four but returned after Mao's death. From there on, Deng consolidated his power and influence by repairing the political, economic, and social damage done by the Cultural Revolution.

Deng's chief interest was in economic reform. He wanted to make China a wealthy and powerful country. To achieve this goal, Deng adopted a policy of opening up China. By that, he meant that China should not cling to the same Marxist strategies. It should look at examples of economically successful countries around the world. As part of this policy, Deng normalized relations (established or restored full diplomatic ties) with Japan and the United States in 1979.

Deng called his plan Socialism with Chinese characteristics. But its capitalist and free-market elements brought him into conflict with the party's old-guard Marxists and Maoists. In response, Deng began political reforms centered on separating party and government organizations at all levels. These reforms limited the extent to which the party could interfere in government decisions, especially regarding local economic reform. And throughout the 1980s, Deng systematically replaced retiring party cadres (officials and administrators) with younger political allies. As these allies filled the top of the party ranks, Deng largely withdrew from his official posts. But he and several other long-standing party members remained very influential. This group, known as the elders, offered advice, approved decisions, and settled disputes within the Politburo. As the leader of the elders, Deng remained the highest authority in the party.

Deng Xiaoping in 1959

Zhao Ziyang *(left)*, premier of the People's Republic of China, and Hu Yaobang *(right)*, general secretary of the Communist Party, were both brought up through the ranks by Deng Xiaoping. Both also agreed with Deng's economic reforms.

Deng's economic policies were successful at first, and Chinese people benefited from a higher standard of living. But over the course of the 1980s, the economy slowed. Inflation (the rising prices of goods and services) increased. People had to stretch their wages to buy necessities. The Chinese people were not used to the ups and downs of a free-market economy, and inflation worried or angered many.

Government corruption was also a common grievance among citizens. Most people dealt with local officials and party members, not with reformers in the highest reaches of power in Beijing. Those local officials were often corrupt and greedy. A successful free-market economy is regulated by rules and standards. These contribute to stability and give people a sense of security when doing business. But China's free-market measures were put into play without these rules and regulations. The average person was at the mercy of unscrupulous business owners or government officials who looked the other way on business crime, awarded contracts and jobs to friends and relatives, and otherwise abused the system.

Most Chinese people remained committed to Socialism and Communism. But they wondered when Deng's reforms would start to show real, long-lasting effects. They began demanding more change from their government, and the loudest and most persistent demands came from university campuses.

CHAPTER 2

BEIJING
AND ITS
STUDENTS

"There is a social malaise [dissatisfaction] in our country today, and the primary reason for it is the poor example set by Party members. Unethical behavior by Party leaders is especially to blame. This is a situation that clearly calls for action on the part of intellectuals."

—Fang Lizhi, in a 1985 speech to Beijing University students

The city of Beijing is more than two thousand years old. It is located in northern China, surrounded by but independent from Hebei Province. Beijing is not the largest city in China (the port city of Shanghai is). But since it became the country's capital in the fifteenth century, Beijing has served as China's political, cultural, and educational center.

CENTRAL BEIJING

In 1402 the Chinese emperor Yongle began building a palace in Beijing. The palace was built in traditional Chinese style but large and grand enough to serve as the earthly home of the son of Heaven. The complex grew to include 980 buildings and courtyards. A wall 33 feet (10 meters) high separates the palace complex from the rest of Beijing. Only the emperor's family and servants were allowed in. Ordinary citizens could not enter, and the complex became known as the Forbidden City.

This modern photograph shows the north entrance to the Forbidden City. The brown roofs are the many buildings that make up the complex.

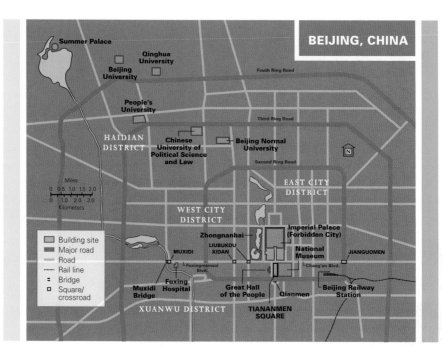

The Forbidden City still stands in central Beijing. It forms the north border of Tiananmen Square, a large, open public area. Chang'an Boulevard runs east-west between the Forbidden City and Tiananmen Square. The square is named after an entryway to the Forbidden City—Tiananmen, or the "Gate of Heavenly Peace."

Just as Beijing is the cultural and political center of China, Tiananmen Square is the heart of Beijing. At 4.7 million square feet (440,000 sq. m), the square is large enough to hold one million people during public gatherings. At the center of the square is a granite column called the Monument to the People's Heroes. Erected in 1952, the column is carved with images from China's modern history.

To the west of the square is the Great Hall of the People, built in 1959. The hall is the site of all official meetings of the CCP and the National People's Congress. Facing the hall across the square is the China National Museum. In the southern part of the square sits Mao Zedong Memorial Hall, the site of Mao's glass coffin. South of that lies Zhengyang Gate, and at the southern edge of the square is the fifteenth-century watchtower called Qianmen.

The Monument to the People's Heroes *(left)* stands at the center of Tiananmen Square. The Zhengyang Gate *(below)*, is at the southern edge of Tiananmen Square.

Zhongnanhai lies to the northwest of Tiananmen Square, alongside the Forbidden City. It was once imperial hunting grounds. But since the founding of the People's Republic, it has served as a government center. The complex contains the offices of the CCP's Central Committee, the State Council, the Central People's Government, and the Military Commission of the Party Central Committee. High-ranking CCP members also have homes within the complex.

BEIJING'S UNIVERSITIES

Some of China's most prestigious higher-learning institutions are in the capital city. Beijing has sixty-seven universities. In the 1980s, those universities had about two hundred thousand students. Most of the universities are in the Haidian District, in the northwest part of the city.

Haidian is home to Qinghua University, the Beijing Institute of Technology, Beijing Normal University (specializing in teacher training), and several other universities. The district's most famous institution is Beijing University. The university is also called Peking University, after an older name for the city. Students call the university Beida.

Beijing University, shown here in 2007, is located in the Haidian District of Beijing. The campus was once imperial parkland.

Beida's 370-acre (150-hectare) campus is home to about ten thousand students. It was established in 1898 as the country's first national university. Nearby is the Summer Palace, which once served as a warm-weather retreat for China's emperors. Most of the university's grounds occupy old imperial parklands. The campus has thick green lawns, mature trees, and traditional Chinese architecture. In the center of campus, the reflection of the slender Treasure Pagoda shimmers in Weiming Lake.

Students read in the grass near the lake, far away from the noise of the city. Some gather around campus statues or other landmarks to discuss sports or culture. Others take a break from studying on the tennis courts. In university dorms, students play cards and games. In the 1980s, mah-jongg (a table game played with tiles similar to dominoes) was especially popular. So was talking politics.

Beida's Democracy Salon was a student organization led by the university's history department. It met in classrooms and on the Cervantes Lawn (an outdoor area of campus) to discuss politics and student issues. Led by student Wang Dan, the salon invited guest speakers, such as scientist and Communist Party critic Li Shuxian, to the university. Students also met and talked politics in another outdoor campus area called the Triangle.

In his book *The Power of Tiananmen*, sociologist Dingxin Zhao points out that the confines of the campus once provided the Maoist government a way to keep an eye on student activism. Government agents would infiltrate the campus, looking and listening for troublemakers. Agents from the Public Security Bureau still kept tabs on student activities in the 1980s. But overall, government control relaxed, and the university's strong sense of community created a protected environment. In this "ecology," as Dingxin calls it, students felt free to exchange ideas and create political networks. Student activist Zhang Boli remembers:

The students of Beijing University were of a mind to exercise their thinking, their passion. A campus wall separated them from the world outside. If you said outside the campus what you said in the classroom, you could be arrested or followed by government spies. The academic atmosphere at Beijing University was amazingly free and informal.

University campuses also provided a platform for planning demonstrations and organizing their participants. Those activities were riskier than merely talking politics in someone's dorm room. But during the 1980s, students believed they had to keep alive the spirit of 1919's May Fourth Movement. Many felt ready to risk government crackdowns for their freedom and for the future of the country.

■■■ STUDENT COMPLAINTS

Many student complaints centered on common themes: freedom, democracy, the loss of status for students and intellectuals, and concern for the future. The students believed that the government's economic and political reforms were not happening fast enough. Deng's promise of a freer and more open society had seemed to result in merely new and different problems.

As part of his plan to modernize China, Deng tried to restore the respect for education that had been lost during the Cultural Revolution. He also wanted students trained in science, law, and other subjects that would benefit a modern economy. Government funding encouraged colleges and universities to expand, and many new ones opened. During the 1980s, the number of Chinese universities almost tripled. Total enrollment doubled.

However, the free-market measures introduced as part of Deng's reform meant that the biggest area of economic growth was in small, private businesses. Those businesses, many family-run, did not need college-educated workers. Foreign firms that set up offices in China brought their own business plans and technology with them. They also did not need China's best and brightest. By the mid-1980s, China had a surplus of scholars and intellectuals. Competition for jobs—even in the government and universities—was fierce, and wages dropped. And what jobs there were, many students believed, went to the sons and daughters, qualified or not, of well-connected CCP members.

In 1988 cases involving economic crime reached record levels in China. More than fifty-five thousand cases were brought to court. More than eight thousand of those cases involved corruption. More than fifteen hundred people were tried for accepting bribes. Almost seventeen hundred were tried for profiteering, a crime that involves taking advantage of people during a crisis (such as a food shortage or a natural disaster) to make an extraordinary profit. Almost two hundred more people were charged with smuggling. The same trend continued into early 1989. Reports from the first three months of that year showed a huge increase in corruption charges brought against government and military leaders.

General crime rates also rose. Reports noted that pickpocketing and robbery rose in the late 1980s. Bandits (robbers who worked in organized groups) operated freely in rural areas. Grave robbing, including the ransacking of ancient burial sites, became widespread. Prostitution and gambling increased. And armed battles between villages and clans (extended family groups) broke out. Many people who had once felt very safe, such as urban students or the elderly, now felt like easy marks for street criminals.

Some security forces believed that many crimes were motivated by people's financial difficulties or by simple greed. Others believed that security throughout the country had weakened because the CCP was not enforcing its Communist ideology. The party had relaxed its hold on Chinese society, but there was nothing to take its place in maintaining social order and security.

Highly respected just a few years before, students and intellectuals felt unappreciated and unneeded. Their social status as intellectuals had protected them from street crime. But they worried that their drop in status made them targets for young street thugs and gang members.

■ DISCONTENT

In reaction to this bleak outlook, many students slacked off. They gave up on the dedicated study routines that had characterized Chinese universities. "There didn't seem to be as much of a reason to study hard," Beida student Shen Tong wrote, "if the government would not let us play a role in shaping the country's future." Some students began skipping class, hanging out with friends, and gambling. Others made plans to leave China after graduation. They studied for English-language exams and applied to foreign universities for graduate school.

On campus, students began ignoring or sidestepping government rules and regulations. They now had a stronger sense of personal freedom. For example, earlier in the decade, universities had started a policy of "lights out" at eleven at night. To discourage students from late-night gatherings, dorms would cut off the power, leaving only dim hall lights on. But students ignored the rule. They simply moved their mah-jongg games and political discussions into the hallways.

Shen Tong was one of many students at Beida frustrated by the lack of respect for intellectuals—and the way the government responded to them.

The air of discontent on campus also gave rise to more radical political ideas. Since Deng had opened China to the rest of the world, students were exposed to Western ideas. They read books about democratic governments.

They heard about civil rights movements and student protests in the United States and Europe. Students and teachers who had studied or worked abroad returned with stories about the personal freedom and optimism that young people in Western countries enjoyed. These stories about the West were often idealized, but the students were inspired by them.

> "We Communist Party members should be open to different ways of thinking. We should be open to different cultures and willing to adopt the elements of those cultures that are clearly superior. A great diversity of thought should be allowed in colleges and universities."
>
> —*Fang Lizhi, in a 1985 speech to Beijing University students*

More than ever before, students began to object to Communist control tactics. As in decades before, universities still prohibited any student organizations not approved by the government. Teachers and members of the Communist Youth League (the young people's organization that led to CCP membership) were still sent out to do political thought work. Thought work involves calling students to formal meetings or engaging them in private conversations to make sure they are "thinking correctly" about Communist ideology. Communist enforcers could report any student activism or even bad attitudes, and that threat still hung over campuses. But more and more, teachers and young enforcers were not interested in turning on their cohorts. They often agreed with student complaints and concerns.

Students became convinced that the government was not being honest about political reforms. The party was still corrupt. There were still too many unelected power brokers, such as the elders, working behind the scenes. Instead of waiting for long-promised change, students began organizing protests to demand change. The first major demonstration of the 1980s occurred in Beijing in the late fall of 1986.

1986 AND ITS AFTERMATH

In the fall of 1986, students in China's Anhui Province began protesting during a local election. The students felt that the CCP was blocking free election campaigns in favor of their chosen candidates. The protests began in the Anhui city of Hefei, led by an astrophysics professor named

BIG-CHARACTER **POSTERS**

Big-character posters—called *dazibao* in Chinese—are handwritten wall posters lettered with large characters. They are meant to be hung in a public place and read by a crowd. The posters were used in China throughout the twentieth century. The government used them to announce CCP programs or to declare official statements on an issue. Citizens used the posters to take part in debates, criticize public figures, or express political opinions. Nongovernmental posters are often anonymous or are signed with pen names, such as the Poor Monk or the Blue Sail.

In 1966 Nie Yuanzi, a student at Beijing University, used a big-character poster to attack university administrators and teachers. She claimed that the university was being run by bourgeois counterrevolutionaries who were working against Chairman Mao. Mao saw Nie's poster and had it read during a national radio broadcast. He then had it published in a national newspaper. Mao's endorsement of the poster is considered by many historians to be the spark that set off the Cultural Revolution. Mao established the use of big-character posters as a constitutionally guaranteed right.

Fang Lizhi (the husband of party critic Li Shuxian, who spoke at Beida's Democracy Salon). Demonstrations spread to Beijing and Shanghai and then to about fifteen other cities. The number of student protesters swelled into the tens of thousands.

As the demonstrations continued, the issues that the students gave voice to expanded. The students called on the government to speed up the pace of democratic reform. They complained about government control of student life—for example, being required to do physical exercises each day or having "lights out" in dorms. The students

Wei Jingsheng first published his 1978 essay, "The Fifth Modernization," as a big-character poster on the Democracy Wall. After the Democracy Wall was closed in 1979, Deng Xiaoping ended the constitutional right to post dazibao. He said that big-character posters and other similar expressions "never played a positive role in China." During the 1980s, students revived the use of big-character posters to express their political discontent.

Chinese citizens read dazibao (big-character posters) for government announcements in the 1950s.

wanted to hold campus elections and be provided more chances to study abroad. Some demanded greater access to Western pop culture, such as music and movies. In general, they wanted more control over their own lives.

The size of the demonstrations shocked government and party officials. The government had lost control of student groups during the Cultural Revolution, and the government didn't want that kind of social upheaval to happen again. Some of the older leaders also condemned the students' demands for Western cultural items. They saw this as "spiritual pollution" and "bourgeois liberalization"—terms the CCP used to describe Western capitalist influences. The CCP regarded these influences as a threat to their cultural and political leadership.

Students returned to their classes in January 1987, and the protests ended. But the effects in government were just beginning. During the demonstrations, Communist Party general secretary Hu Yaobang had refused to condemn the students. In the aftermath, he was criticized for not stopping the demonstrations before they spread. He was even accused of supporting bourgeois liberalization. On January 16, he was forced to resign in disgrace from political office.

The CCP appointed Zhao Ziyang as new general secretary. Li Peng was made premier. Li was unpopular with the people, especially young people. But he was a hard-line supporter of Communist policy and therefore valuable to the government.

With Deng's encouragement, the government also launched an Anti-Spiritual Pollution Campaign

Li Peng became premier of China in January 1987. His hard-line politics made him unpopular with most young people.

and an Anti-Bourgeois Liberalization Campaign. The campaigns insisted that Western-style reforms were not the answer to China's problems. China, the CCP said, must stick to the Four Modernizations in promoting economic reform. The party was committed to political reform too, but not at a pace that would invite economic instability.

The government remained faithful to its Communist ideology. And the students held to their demands for political reform. On campus, student activists became more vocal. Protests took place throughout the mid and late 1980s. But these protests were smaller than the 1986 demonstrations. Students were waiting for the right moment to mount a larger protest. That moment arrived in the spring of 1989.

CHAPTER 3

CLASH

*Li Peng, come out!
Li Peng, come out!"*

—Student protesters at Beijing's Xinhua Gate and
the Great Hall of the People, April 1989

On April 8, 1989, former CCP leader Hu Yaobang attended a government committee meeting. During the meeting, comrades noticed that he was pale and had trouble paying attention. He finally rose to excuse himself but collapsed to the floor. Comrades knelt around him while waiting for an ambulance. He was taken to the hospital and treated for a massive heart attack. For a few days, he seemed to be recovering. But early in the morning on April 15, Hu died.

The news hit hard among Beijing students. Students gathered on city campuses to discuss Hu's death. They were truly sad about his passing. But they were also angry. They felt that the stress of Hu's resignation and disgrace had caused his heart attack. They blamed the leadership of the CCP, especially Deng and hard-liner Li Peng.

Students admired Hu's refusal to condemn the 1986 student protesters. Hu had become a symbol of true reform and of a clean and transparent (honest and accessible) government. "There seemed to be an outpouring of emotion over what he had come to represent," Beida student Shen Tong recalled. "To honor him at the time of his death was a way of challenging the current Party hierarchy." Feng Congde, a graduate student at Beida, agreed: "In Chinese culture, there's a phenomenon I'd call the cult of the dead. After death, all the man's flaws are forgotten and his memory is enshrined in a halo of glory. Then people use the dead man to vent their anger and express their hopes." Students began writing dazibao praising Hu and criticizing the way the party had treated him. Many also began making memorial flower wreaths to bring to Tiananmen Square.

DEMONSTRATIONS BEGIN

Politburo members discussed Hu's death. Zhao Ziyang urged the CCP to give Hu a state funeral (a public memorial service reserved for important figures). The Politburo members agreed. But Zhao and others were worried that students would use the public funeral as an opportunity to publicize other complaints. As plans for the April 22 funeral were announced on CCTV, security forces were told to monitor any disturbances or unusual activities, especially on campuses.

On April 17, spontaneous memorials to Hu took place on twenty-six Beijing campuses. Government reports noted that students had gathered in areas such as Beida's Triangle. The participants were young—mostly first- and second-year students. And they were "shouting and highly emotional." The reports noted that activities had already turned from mourning Hu to complaining about how he was treated by the CCP and then to wider social grievances. Similar reports arrived from a few other large cities, such as Shanghai.

The Politburo met and discussed the reports. Zhao stated that the government should acknowledge the students' grief and patriotism but appeal to them to be reasonable and peaceful. Hard-liner Li Peng argued that the demonstrations should be stopped at once before they got out of hand. Li believed that the student movement had already been infiltrated by anti-Communist agitators.

In Beijing, student mourners began moving off campuses to converge on Tiananmen Square. About six hundred students and teachers from the Chinese University of Political Science and Law carried memorial banners and wreaths to the square. They laid a flower wreath at the base of the Monument to the People's Heroes. As the day wore on, more students marched to the square. They began shouting political slogans. Foreign news reporters and Beijing residents gathered to watch. The police encouraged people to move on. But the crowd reached ten thousand people by late afternoon. Speeches and poetry recitations continued into the evening. About three hundred people stayed through the night.

Before dawn on April 18, about one thousand students set out from Beida. Wang Dan, Zhang Boli, Guo Haifeng, and several other student activists led the way. They carried banners and marched in a procession through the streets. Along the way, they sang the "Internationale," a Communist anthem sung in many countries.

At an intersection west of the city center, the marchers encountered about one hundred armed police officers. Zhang stepped forward to explain that the students were going to pay their respects to Hu. The police commander replied that he would not stop them but that they had to use another route. They could not march past a hotel filled with foreign guests. Zhang recalled that as the students marched on, many of the police officers smiled and waved. Shen Tong remembers walking through six police barricades. He said that each time, the police stepped aside, as if knowing that they could not stop the huge wave of marchers.

The Beida procession reached Tiananmen Square at about four in the morning. Student leaders met at the heroes' monument, surrounded by the other marchers. Zhang Boli and others announced that students were forming their own autonomous (student-run and not under official control) organizations. They had drawn up a petition, or list, of demands and would send elected student leaders to negotiate with the government.

The petition included seven items. The list had grown out of common student grievances. It also included some basic civil rights— such as freedom of the press and freedom of assembly. The seven demands were that the government should

1. reevaluate its treatment of Hu Yaobang and announce that his views on democracy had been correct;
2. end the campaigns against spiritual pollution and bourgeois liberalization;
3. publish the salaries and other assets of government leaders and their families;
4. end government censorship of the press and allow the publication of privately run newspapers;
5. increase government spending on higher education and increase wages for intellectuals;
6. end government restrictions on demonstrations in Beijing;
7. hold democratic elections to replace corrupt or ineffective government officials who had been appointed by the CCP.

Students also wanted official media to broadcast the petition and, in general, provide fair and impartial coverage of the student movement.

In 1980 reformers within the Chinese government wanted a publication that would promote their ideas and arguments for political and economic change. They turned to editor Qin Benli. Qin had been denounced as a rightist (elitist and capitalist) during the 1950s and had been blacklisted from journalism for two decades. With the reformers' support, he began publishing the *World Economic Herald* in Shanghai.

The *Herald* was not an official, party-approved newspaper. The CCP tolerated the *Herald*, although it would not allow the paper to print an English-language edition. The paper was often the target of government hard-liners in the 1980s. But its coverage of dissident politics and corruption issues gained the respect of many Chinese intellectuals.

On April 19, four days after Hu Yaobang's death, editor Qin began hosting roundtable forums with leading intellectuals. The forums were held in honor of Hu, but the intellectuals also discussed democratic reforms and the growing student movement. They were often highly critical of the government. On April 21, Qin began preparing a long story about the discussions for publication in the *Herald*'s April 24 issue. The head of the CCP in Shanghai, Jiang Zemin, heard of the plans. He demanded to see the paper prior to publication. After reviewing the story, Jiang told Qin to remove several offending paragraphs and some photos of the student demonstrations. Qin refused and sent the paper to the printer.

The next day, Jiang confiscated all printed copies of the newspaper. On April 26, he removed Qin from his position on the paper. Jiang and the CCP took over publication of the *Herald*. On April 27, party supervisors fired the *Herald* staff. The April 24 issues were reprinted without the

Chinese journalists sign a letter condemning the dismissal of Qin Benli from the *World Economic Herald* in 1989.

photos of student demonstrators. And in place of the controversial paragraphs, the party inserted official government statements.

Intellectuals and students in Beijing soon got word of the Herald takeover. Demonstrators in Beijing, Shanghai, and other cities demanded that Qin be reinstated as editor and that the Herald be allowed to publish freely. The Herald controversy drew Chinese journalists into the 1989 student movement.

■ XINHUA GATE INCIDENT

In another part of the square, several hundred students gathered in front of the Great Hall of the People. They began a sit-in—a demonstration in which participants simply sit down and refuse to move. Student leaders joined the sit-in with their petition. The group demanded that high-ranking government officials come out, talk to the students, and accept the list of demands. In the early evening, some lower-ranking officials appeared. They met with Guo Haifeng and Wang Dan and promised to let their superiors know about the petition.

The student protesters were not satisfied. About eleven at night, two thousand students left the Great Hall. They began walking down Chang'an Boulevard to Zhongnanhai, the walled complex where Zhao Ziyang, Li Peng, and other CCP leaders had homes and offices.

Early the next day, April 19, students staged a sit-in at the Xinhua Gate, the main entrance to Zhongnanhai on Chang'an Boulevard. The sit-in demonstrators were joined by students on their way to Tiananmen Square and by many curious onlookers. The crowd grew to about ten thousand. The demonstrators sang the "Internationale" and shouted, "Long live democracy" and "Down with autocracy." They shouted their loyalty to Hu and to the spirit of the May Fourth Movement.

Meanwhile, students continued to gather in Tiananmen Square. They carried floral wreaths, school flags, and hand-printed banners. By evening about four thousand students and fifteen thousand onlookers filled the square around the heroes' monument. Beijing city officials sent one thousand police officers to the square to keep order. The city government also announced that starting the next day, security forces would surround the monument. The Communist Youth League would handle the presentation of wreaths.

Later in the evening, some of the students returned to their campuses. Still, a few thousand people remained in the square. When a large group tried to leave the square to join the Xinhua Gate sit-in demonstrators, the police stopped them. Police were already trying to break up the sit-in, and they did not want anyone else moving toward Zhongnanhai.

A student reads a poem from the heroes' monument in Tiananmen Square on April 19, 1989. The banner behind him shows Hu Yaobang, whose funeral began the student demonstrations.

At Xinhua Gate, police stood in a line and linked arms to form a cordon to separate the three hundred sit-in protesters from the onlookers. Most of the onlookers gradually left the area. Police then took up positions between the remaining students and the gate. Through the night, students shouted, "Li Peng, come out!" They tried several times to break through the police line. Some threw rocks and bottles at officers.

At about five in the morning on April 20, Beijing officials sent buses to the site to carry the students back to campus. They ordered police to load students onto the bus—by force if needed. Some students refused to go, and fights broke out between students and officers. Police eventually cleared the area.

When the students got back to campus, some held up bloodstained shirts. Others had injuries to their faces. They said that they had been beaten by the police. Wuer Kaixi, a first-year student at Beijing Normal,

The Xinhua Gate (above) is the entrance to Zhongnanhai, the headquarters of the CCP.

got up in front of a crowd of students and announced that "about one thousand police and soldiers brutally broke into our ranks. They savagely beat us up. They also beat up other citizens."

Rumors of police brutality toward the sit-in demonstrators spread quickly among students. One Beijing University student later said, "This made us very angry. Demonstration is a constitutional right."

The government got wind of the rumors and denied police brutality. Officials said that some students had injured themselves breaking windows on the buses. But the students did not believe the government. They began calling the police skirmish the Xinhua Gate Bloody Incident.

Student leaders called for class boycotts and more demonstrations. At Beida, student activists formed the Beida Solidarity Student Union Preparatory Committee to organize activities and coordinate with other schools. Together, the schools planned to form an Autonomous Federation of Students. Student leaders began collecting donations on campus and from people on the street. They used the money to buy megaphones and supplies for armbands, headbands, posters, and leaflets.

A COMRADE'S FUNERAL

Behind the red walls of Zhongnanhai, the Politburo monitored the situation. After the Xinhua Gate Bloody Incident, Zhao was concerned for security and public order. But he seemed unconvinced that anti-government forces were organizing the demonstrations. Deng, Li Peng, and others believed organized agitators were behind the shouts of "Down with autocracy." They pointed out that some students were beginning to shout, "Down with the Communist Party."

The Politburo worried that support for the students and general anger at corruption would convince factory workers to join the protests. Striking factory workers could deal a blow to China's economy. To stem the spread of demonstrations, the Politburo decided to first try political tactics. University administrators, business and factory managers, and local government officials were reminded to publish party proclamations, enforce rules, and do political thought work among employees and students.

On April 21, Beijing officials announced that Tiananmen Square would be closed for Hu's funeral at the Great Hall of the People. At the same time, student activists sent messages to campuses across the city, asking students to meet at Beijing Normal University. By evening, students from more than twenty universities had joined the Beijing Normal rally. At ten, the crowds began a march toward Tiananmen. More students joined them along the way, and the procession swelled

Soldiers form a line between student protesters and the Great Hall of the People during the funeral of Hu Yaobang on April 22, 1989.

to about fifty thousand students. At the square, they joined more students and citizens already there. Students from other Chinese cities also began arriving in Beijing by train and making their way to the square. Some estimates suggest that the total was close to two hundred thousand people.

Very early on April 22, Beijing police officers arrived at the Great Hall of the People. They formed a cordon between the hall and the crowds. Government officials came out of the hall and tried to convince students to move back to the heroes' monument during the funeral.

Students refused, saying that they were there to see the funeral. To ease the situation, officials took five student representatives into the hall to discuss issues. The students emerged with the news that the memorial service would be broadcast over the square's loudspeaker system and that the students' view would not be blocked by funeral traffic. Satisfied, some students moved back toward the monument. But others remained close to the police cordon.

Deng, Zhao, Li Peng, and other senior leaders arrived at about ten in the morning for the funeral. Zhao gave the funeral speech. He praised Hu as a "loyal, tried, and tested Communist fighter." But he did not, as the students wanted, affirm that Hu's attitude toward the 1986 student demonstrations had been correct.

After the funeral, Zhao met with Deng. Zhao was leaving the next day for an official state visit to North Korea. He did not want to draw international attention to the current demonstrations by canceling a state visit. But he wanted to discuss plans with Deng before he left. He explained to Deng that he believed that students must be convinced to return to classes and to their normal routines. The police must avoid any kind of violence, and demonstrators should only be punished if they break a law, such as vandalism or assault. Media reports should include positive aspects of the student movement. Zhao also voiced the opinion that the government should begin dialogues with student leaders to address the concerns that had led to the protests. Deng agreed, and Zhao then met with Politburo members and other elders to relay the information. While Zhao was in North Korea, Li Peng would be in charge of party business.

KNEELING AT THE GREAT HALL

With the funeral over and senior leaders still inside the Great Hall, student leaders decided to again present their list of seven demands. Wuer Kaixi wanted to rush inside the Great Hall with the petition. Zhang Boli disagreed. "In a democratic country," he said, "no one should burst into a government building just to act out his anger or resentment." Zhang suggested that, instead, student representatives kneel on the steps of the hall with the petition. Kneeling with a government petition was a traditional act in China. Kneeling would show respect. Wuer argued that they would be kowtowing—bowing to the ground as if begging before their betters.

Zhang's suggestion prevailed, and four student leaders were chosen. Zhou Yongjun, Guo Haifeng, Zhang Boli, and Wuer Kaixi pushed their way through the police cordon to the front of the Great Hall. Zhou, Guo, and Zhang dropped to their knees on the steps. Wuer stood behind them. Guo held the petition over his head. Government staff appeared, and the four asked to see Li Peng. The staff members offered to take the petition to Li, but the students refused. They insisted on speaking directly to Li. The staff members disappeared back inside.

Twenty minutes passed. The crowd was growing angry. Wuer Kaixi took an electronic amplifier and asked why the premier of the people would not come and talk to them. The crowd began to chant, "Li Peng, come out." Some students pushed at the police cordon, and the police pushed back. More time passed, and the chants turned to, "Down with Li Peng!"

Many Beijing workers had come to the square for the funeral, and they watched the kneeling students with sympathy. Worker Lü Jinghua felt that Li Peng should have, at the very least, come out to accept the petition. "[Li] completely ignored the students," Lü said. "Now how do you expect people to take that?"

By midafternoon it was clear that Li would not accept the petition. The students gave up. Feeling insulted and angry, they left the square. They returned to their campuses but not to classes. The boycott had begun.

CHAPTER 4

TURMOIL

> Party organization at all levels, all the members of the Party, of the Youth League . . . , all patriots must differentiate right from wrong, must stand firm and eliminate the turmoil resolutely and immediately."
>
> —*People's Daily* editorial accusing the student movement of creating political and social turmoil and endangering the country, April 26, 1989

After Hu's funeral, the government emphasized to university administrators that campus life must return to normal. Class schedules must resume, and midterm exams must be held on time. If students are emotional, teachers and staff must calm them. If students are hearing rumors, teachers and staff must help them separate fact from fiction.

Students, however, had their own plans. At seventeen major universities in Beijing, students were planning boycotts. From undergraduates to doctoral candidates, students announced that they would refuse to attend classes until May 4, the anniversary of the 1919 student demonstrations. The boycotters would demand that the government and the CCP make anticorruption reforms. They would also demand that students be free to form autonomous organizations on campus. At some universities, students began printing independent newspapers to circulate news of the movement. At other schools, students took over the radio stations and public broadcast systems.

A DECLARATION OF WAR

The Politburo discussed these campus activities with mounting anger. With Zhao out of the country, Li Peng led the discussions. He called some of the student demands "a naked declaration of war against the Party." Beijing's mayor, Chen Xitong, agreed. So did senior party official Li Ximing. They argued their case to Deng Xiaoping.

At a meeting on April 24, Mayor Chen reported that almost fifty thousand students at thirty-nine schools were boycotting classes. The student movement was gaining sympathy and support among citizens and workers. "The students themselves would not be able to come up with this kind of power," Li Ximing is reported to have said. "Black hands and provocateurs [people secretly working to cause political unrest] are behind them." Chen showed Deng a report of students at Beijing Normal shouting, "Down with Deng Xiaoping" and other specific insults about CCP officials.

Deng's plans for economic reform were based on a freer and more open society. He was reluctant to disturb those plans by taking a hard line against students—the country's future scientists, teachers, and party members. But he agreed with Li Peng and the others. He thought the student demonstrations were turning into an antigovernment movement. The CCP and the education system, the Politburo believed, had failed to enforce party ideology among students. Without strong Communist training, the students were being easily led by antigovernment troublemakers. As a result, social stability was in jeopardy.

The Politburo had another concern. It had received a report that students had changed their boycott plans. They were no longer planning to end the boycott on May 4. Instead, they would continue until their demands for dialogue were met. Mikhail Gorbachev was scheduled to arrive in Beijing on May 15 for a state (an official government) visit.

GORBACHEV

In 1989 the Soviet Union was a Communist country. As in other Communist nations, one party ruled the government and citizens lacked political and economic freedoms. Communist rule and the expense of the Cold War (the hostilities with Western nations, 1945–1991) had damaged education, technological development, and the economy in the Soviet Union.

However, beginning in 1986, Mikhail Gorbachev had been pursuing two major policies of change—glasnost and perestroika. Glasnost was a campaign to ease political repression at home and open diplomatic relations with the West. Perestroika focused on economic reforms that would stimulate the Soviet economy. Because of glasnost and perestroika, Chinese students saw Gorbachev as a reformer and possible ally of their pro-democracy movement.

Gorbachev was the general secretary of the Communist Party of the Soviet Union. Relations between China and the Soviet Union had been strained for decades. This was the first time in thirty years that a Soviet leader was paying a state visit to China. The historic visit would be covered by media outlets from all over the world. Beijing would be filled with foreign reporters and photographers. Deng did not want foreign investors and governments to see China wracked by protests. The Chinese government wanted the student demonstrations to end well before Gorbachev arrived.

■ THE APRIL 26 EDITORIAL

On April 25, party leadership wrote an editorial about the Tiananmen Square demonstrations and campus unrest. The editorial was written by the party's propaganda department and approved by Li Peng and Deng. It accused a small group of subversives (those who try to overthrow the government) of using Hu Yaobang's death as an excuse to cause political trouble and "plunge the whole country into chaos." Further, it accused this group of illegally plotting to overthrow the government:

> After [Hu's funeral], an extremely small number of people with ulterior purposes continued to take advantage of the young students' feelings of grief for Comrade Hu Yaobang to spread all kinds of rumors to poison and confuse people's minds. Using both big- and small-character posters, they vilified [abused], hurled invectives [insults] at, and attacked party and state leaders. Blatantly violating the Constitution, they called for opposition to the leadership by the Communist Party and the socialist system.

The editorial called for all Chinese people to recognize the seriousness of this antigovernment conspiracy and to take action to halt it. Illegal organizations and demonstrations should be stopped. People spreading antigovernment rumors should be criminally punished. Students should be prevented from visiting other campuses and factories. The editorial was broadcast on CCTV the evening of April 25.

It was published in the *People's Daily* the next day. The article became known as the April 26 editorial.

Students across Beijing and beyond were outraged by the editorial. A key factor in the students' reaction was that the editorial used the word *dongluan*—Chinese for "turmoil" or "chaos." It was a word often used to describe the violence and mayhem of the Cultural Revolution.

The students understood that the editorial had come from the highest level of the CCP. Some saw it as an implicit threat. By labeling the student movement antigovernment turmoil and claiming that it was endangering national security, the CCP was announcing that it would repress—by any means necessary—further student activity. But the vast majority of students took the editorial as an insult. They felt that they had a constitutional right to demonstrate. Their honesty and loyalty to China was being questioned. Instead of being compared to the patriotic May Fourth Movement students of 1919, they were being compared to the Red Guards.

Before the editorial's publication, students had begun to weary of daily protests. Student leaders tried to keep up the movement's momentum with speeches and rallies. But students were beginning to drift back to classes and normal routines. However, "the editorial created an explosive reaction that pushed the student movement to a new high." On April 27, fifty thousand Beijing students from more than forty universities marched to Tiananmen Square to protest the editorial. Demonstrations also took place in Shanghai, Nanjing, and other major cities.

The Beijing demonstrations were peaceful and orderly, and students were careful to avoid provocative language. They sang traditional Communist songs and proclaimed their loyalty to their country. The students' words and behavior garnered sympathy from Beijing citizens and workers. They took up the students' complaint that the April 26 editorial was unfair and unhelpful. Newspaper editors complained that they wanted to report honestly on what the students were doing, rather than just parroting party rhetoric (language). Even police and soldiers sent to Tiananmen to monitor the demonstrations seemed sympathetic to the students.

On April 28, Li Peng had to publish another *People's Daily* editorial. This one emphasized that the previous editorial had only been attacking "people with hidden intentions." It urged all innocent and patriotic students to avoid these troublemakers and go back to classes. The country's stability, it said, was on the line.

Party leadership followed that editorial with a notice sent throughout the education system. School and university officials were urged to calm things down on their campuses. Teachers and Communist Youth League members were urged to step up political thought work. Party strategy was to divide and conquer—separate the mass of moderate students from the more radical element, disband illegal campus organizations, and cover up the student movement posters with party propaganda.

THE BLACK HANDS

Early in the Tiananmen confrontation, government officials began claiming that only a small group was leading the antigovernment demonstrations. Most students, the government said, were patriotic and had good intentions. But they were allowing themselves to be led astray by the "black hand" of anti-Communists agitators and foreign agents hostile to the Chinese government.

In using such terms, the government was attempting to undercut the movement's cohesiveness. It wanted to encourage student demonstrators to distance themselves from activists such as astrophysics professor Fang Lizhi and from more radical student leaders such as Wang Dan. The government's rhetoric also implied that only this small knot of troublemakers would be punished, while patriotic students would face no consequences.

■ FIRST DIALOGUE

Internally, party leaders argued among themselves. Some believed that the students were merely emotional and idealistic. The believed if the government opened dialogues, the students could be persuaded to stay loyal to the party. Other officials expressed shame that corruption had lowered party status this far. But Li Peng and the hard-liners maintained their position that anti-China forces were behind the student movement. They were outraged that students were talking to foreign reporters and drawing support from the KMT in Taiwan.

Still, to pacify students, Li Peng scheduled a dialogue session for April 29. Yuan Mu, a State Council representative, presided over the session. He and three other officials met with forty-five students. Most of the students were chosen from official university organizations. During the dialogue, students asked questions and the officials responded. When asked about corruption, Yuan replied that the government was dealing with specific cases as they were reported. When asked about press censorship, Yuan replied, "There is no such thing." When asked

DUIHUA

During the 1989 student movement, the word duihua—"dialogue"—was often heard. In political circles, dialogue between the government and the people was a fairly new concept. Previously, the CCP had dismissed the idea as something only Western governments needed. In China, they claimed, the party already spoke for the people, so there was no need for dialogue. But in the 1980s, Zhao Ziyang pushed for dialogue as an element of political reform. In 1987 Zhao convinced the party to formally adopt a policy of being open to dialogue. But in 1989, CCP hard-liners still regarded duihua and negotiation as a weak attempt to imitate Western culture and as an obstacle to party leadership.

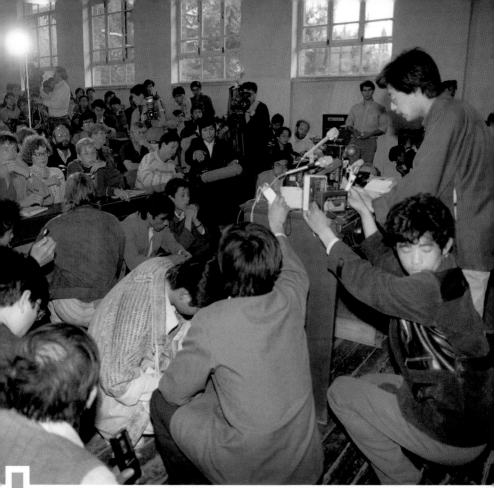

Chinese students meet with government officials on April 29, 1989, to ask questions.

why Hu Yaobang had been driven from office, Yuan said that Hu had admitted his own mistakes and resigned. Student delegates did not argue with the officials' answers, and the dialogue ended.

The government had agreed to broadcast the dialogue, and that evening, students around the country heard it on CCTV. Listeners immediately began complaining that the preapproved student delegates had asked only "softball" questions. Student leaders such as Wang Dan and Wuer Kaixi "rejected the dialogue as phony." Daizabo appeared on campuses criticizing the government's dishonesty, and students in twenty-three cities demonstrated.

Several Beijing universities were heavily involved in the 1989 demonstrations—Beida, the University of Political Science and Law, Beijing Normal, and others. Each of these institutions had its own student leaders. But over the course of the demonstrations, several students emerged as leaders on Tiananmen Square. Some of these leaders were drawn to the political and organizational side of the movement. Others were willing to take the lead on the square and talk to the media. Others were charismatic speakers.

Who were some of these student leaders mentioned most frequently in accounts of the demonstrations? Wang Dan (*below left*) was a twenty-year-old history student at Beida in 1989. Chai Ling was a twenty-three-year-old graduate student studying child psychology at Beijing Normal. Her husband, Feng Congde, was twenty-two and studying physics at Beida. At twenty-nine, Zhang Boli had worked as a journalist and was doing graduate work at Beida. Wuer Kaixi (*far right*) was a twenty-one-year-old student at Beijing Normal.

■ ZHAO RETURNS

When Zhao Ziyang returned from North Korea on April 30, he took time to catch up on developments in the student movement. Reports indicated that in Beijing, almost 70 percent of university students were boycotting classes. Other major cities reported that student demonstrations were increasing and that almost half of the college population was on strike. Reports also indicated that foreign media were closely following the student movement in China. Major television networks and newspapers in the United States and Europe were increasing coverage of demonstrations and taking an editorial stand in favor of the students.

On May 1, the Politburo Standing Committee met. The committee was divided along familiar lines. Zhao thought the government should answer student concerns about political reform. Li Peng argued that the demonstrations must be put down and order restored. Mayor Chen Xitong and others expressed their belief that the demonstrations would not peter out after the May Fourth anniversary had passed. The students were, they said, planning for a long battle. Zhao still insisted on the patriotic and legal motivations of the students. But at the end of the meeting, he agreed to focus on national stability.

The next day, seventy students from more than forty schools met at Beida. They began organizing a Beijing Student Dialogue Delegation. The delegation finalized a petition demanding that the government set up a series of dialogues with students. The petition specified that students themselves would decide who represented them at the dialogues. Neither the government nor official campus organizations could interfere. Delegates took the petition to a government office, and from there, it was forwarded to the Politburo Standing Committee.

At a press conference on May 3, Yuan Mu, who presided over the earlier dialogue, rejected the student petition. He said that the Dialogue Delegation was an illegal organization. It was trying to unfairly exclude official campus organizations that represented a majority of students. Yuan also argued that dialogues should be made in good faith, without threats and conditions.

Later that day, Zhao Ziyang made a speech emphasizing the importance of national stability and public order. But he also praised student demonstrators and their opposition to corruption. Students reacted angrily to Yuan's words, but they were encouraged by Zhao's speech. As a concession to Zhao's speech, student leaders announced that they would demonstrate on May 4 but return to class May 5.

MAY 4

Across China, official and unofficial celebrations marked the seventieth anniversary of the May Fourth Movement. Students demonstrated in fifty-one cities. In Beijing tens of thousands of students left their campuses at about eight in the morning. They were joined by about two hundred journalists. They marched to Tiananmen Square from three directions, carrying banners, singing, and chanting slogans. The student demonstrators overwhelmed the official government celebrations.

In the afternoon, leaders from the autonomous student federation read a "May Fourth Declaration." The declaration emphasized the student movement's commitment to China's modernization through democracy, the rule of law, and a respect for human rights. The federation announced that students would return to classes but would continue their campaign for dialogue with the government. How the government reacted to the demands for dialogue, students said, would determine the future of student demonstrations.

As students demonstrated in Tiananmen, Zhao Ziyang conducted government business. He met with leaders of the Asian Development Bank (ADB), a group that encourages foreign investments in Asian countries. At the meeting, Zhao spoke at length about the student demonstrations. If there is an antigovernment element within the movement, he said, it is small and it is not leading the movement. Zhao said he was confident that the vast majority of the students were not opposed to the Communist leadership. Student concerns with corruption and democracy matched the party's concerns with the same issues. Zhao repeated his belief that the demonstrations and unrest could be solved through dialogue and the exchange of ideas.

After the ADB meeting, Zhao met with Li Peng. Li Peng praised Zhao's speech and said he would take the same tack when he met with ADB delegates the next day. Talk then turned to the April 26 *People's Daily* editorial. Zhao explained that he believed that the party must take steps to repair the damage done by the editorial's tone. The tone, Zhao said, had alienated people and added to the nationwide unrest. He suggested that the party leadership revise the editorial. Li Peng disagreed. He reminded Zhao that the editorial reflected the sentiments of the Politburo, including Deng. "We can't possibly change the core message." The two leaders left the meeting without reaching an agreement.

THE HUNGER STRIKE DECLARATION

Zhao's meeting with the Asian Development Bank was nationally televised. Local party officials around China reacted to the speech. Some were confused. Zhao's speech seemed to contradict the April 26 editorial, and officials wondered which party line they were supposed to enforce. Was it turmoil that threatened the state, or wasn't it? Many party officials agreed with Zhao's position.

Within the Politburo Standing Committee, Zhao continued to argue for softening the April 26 editorial. He asked Chinese president Yang Shangkun to bring the matter up with Deng. Yang did, and Zhao followed up with his own meeting with Deng. Deng listened to Zhao's arguments. If it would clear the students off the

Yang Shangkun was the president of the People's Republic of China from 1988 to 1993.

square before Gorbachev's visit, Deng was willing to consider revising the editorial.

Meanwhile, many students began to return to class. Students from several universities had been demonstrating in support of freedom of the press. But in many places, the movement seemed to be winding down. Some student leaders, such as Wang Dan, recognized that students were tired. The movement, Wang thought, was entering a new stage. "No more large-scale, intense street action, no more boycotting classes," Wang told a Canadian reporter on May 10. "Instead, we need down-to-earth work to build democracy on campus." Wang wanted to continue work on establishing autonomous organizations and student-run news media.

But soon after telling the reporter this, on May 11, Wang met with Wuer Kaixi and a few other students for dinner. They discussed their mistrust of the government. They did not believe that the government wanted to hold dialogues. They thought that party leaders were playing for time, waiting for the movement to die out. The CCP was also sticking to its position of regarding the student movement as antigovernment turmoil. That meant that any student demonstrator could be accused of a political crime. The government couldn't arrest tens of thousands of student demonstrators. But if the movement dwindled down to only a few leaders, those few could easily be arrested. The next stage, the students decided, would have to be radical enough to reenergize the movement and force the government to accept student demands. The group proposed a hunger strike—a refusal to eat any food until demands are met. They took their idea to other student leaders such as Chai Ling (a Beida graduate student); her husband, Feng Congde; and Zhang Boli. They all agreed.

On May 12, government officials announced that they were ready to hold the first in a series of dialogues. But the student federation was caught up in its own arguments. Some federation leaders objected to the idea of a hunger strike. They wanted to take a moderate approach and wanted to show a compromising spirit by not demonstrating during Gorbachev's visit. But Feng Congde, Chai Ling, Wang Dan, Wuer Kaixi, and others disregarded the objections. The unity of the student leadership began to fray.

A "Hunger Strike Declaration" was posted at Beijing University. At first, only about forty Beida students signed up for the hunger strike. On the evening of May 12, the hunger strike faction met at the Triangle. As students gathered around, Chai made an emotional speech. The hunger strike, she said, would force the government to show its true face. But the hunger strike would also give students a chance "to see whether the people have a conscience or not, to see if China still has a conscience or not, if it has hope or not." After the speech, about three hundred students joined the strike.

> **The country is our country.**
> **The people are our people.**
> **The government is our government.**
> **Who will shout if not us?**
> **Who will act if not us?**
> —Hunger Strike Declaration, May 12, 1989

THE HUNGER STRIKE BEGINS

The government learned of the planned hunger strike early on May 13. The news rippled through government leadership. Deng and the hard-liners were outraged that the students would try to embarrass the country during Gorbachev's visit. Zhao Ziyang was dismayed. He had assured Deng that the students could be persuaded to stay away from the square during the visit. But the students had upped their tactics.

Yan Mingfu called an emergency meeting with intellectuals and student leaders. Yan was a member of the CCP's Central Committee and government minister of the United Front Department, an office that maintained links with ethnic minorities, intellectuals, and other groups outside of the Communist mainstream. Yan was a political moderate and an ally of Zhao Ziyang. Yan hoped that the intellectuals could persuade the students to abandon the hunger strike before Gorbachev's arrival. He feared that Li Peng and the hard-liners would use the situation to convince Deng that Zhao's moderate position was not working. The intellectuals shared that fear and agreed to Yan's plan.

Wuer Kaixi, Shen Tong, Wang Dan, Chai Ling, Feng Congde, and other student leaders arrived at the meeting at about five in the afternoon on May 13. They were not sure why the meeting was being held by the United Front. Shen Tong concluded that Yan was simply the only high-ranking official interested in talking to students.

Chai and Feng left the meeting soon after it began, possibly because Chai was exhausted from organizing the hunger strike. The remaining student leaders told Yan that they wanted the government to publicly acknowledge that the student movement was patriotic, not illegal. They wanted immediate dialogues with government leaders on key issues, and they wanted the dialogues to be broadcast live on national TV.

Yan replied that he understood the students' suspicions about the government actions. He assured them that their actions were legal and that he would take their demands to the Central Committee. But he asked them to consider China's reputation during Gorbachev's historic visit. The students appreciated Yan's honesty and agreed to leave Tiananmen Square by May 15.

While the meeting was going on that day, the three hundred hunger strikers gathered at Beida. They put on white headbands and took an oath to not break their fast until the movement's goals had been met. They ate a final meal bought by some teachers. Then they set off for the square. At Tiananmen they were joined by a few thousand supporters—students, citizens, and some first-aid workers. That night the temperatures dropped to 41°F (5°C). The strike had been hastily planned, and most students had arrived wearing only street clothes. Beijing residents began bringing blankets, sleeping bags, and hot water to drink.

ANOTHER FAILED DIALOGUE

On Sunday, May 14, the crowd at Tiananmen Square swelled to thirty thousand. The government decided not to greet Gorbachev at

争自由

HUNGER STRIKE FOR FREEDOM

Students on a hunger strike wear headbands and hold a banner to proclaim their message.

Tiananmen Square. CCP leaders would meet him at Beijing's airport instead. Deng and other Politburo members were outraged. Not only had the students refused to consider China's national image, some had sent a petition to Gorbachev asking to meet the Russian leader. In a Politburo meeting, hard-liners told Deng that the party is speaking with two voices—Zhao Ziyang's and Li Peng's. They argued that the students had sensed and were trying to exploit a rift in government leadership.

Late in the afternoon, student leaders again met Yan Mingfu and his aides. While foreign and Chinese newspaper reporters milled around outside the United Front offices, a CCTV crew set up cameras in a conference room. But officials explained to the students that the dialogue could not be broadcast live. CCTV had already scheduled a soccer game broadcast. The dialogue would be recorded live and broadcast later. The students agreed to that on the condition that an audiotape of the meeting be carried live over loudspeakers in Tiananmen Square. The student dialogue delegates wanted students outside to be assured that this dialogue was not a repeat of the "phony" April 29 meeting.

The students and government began the dialogue at six in the evening The students had chosen only thirteen delegates to speak, to make sure speakers kept to the agenda. Those thirteen sat at the conference tables with officials while the other students stood in back. But soon, students began passing numerous notes to the speakers, telling them what to ask next. The dialogue became a series of questions, many unrelated to the agenda. In addition, aides began passing notes to officials. "I could tell something was going on outside," student leader Shen Tong recalled. "The atmosphere was very tense."

Suddenly, a group of students burst into the conference, struggling to get past security guards. They demanded that the meeting be stopped. The audiotape was not being broadcast in the square as promised, and students outside took this as a sign that delegates were cutting some sort of deal with the government.

The student delegates repeatedly asked Yan what had happened to the broadcast. But it seemed clear that Yan was unaware of the situation. Without the broadcast, the meeting ended. Some students, such as Shen Tong, believed that someone in the Politburo had stopped the broadcast without telling Yan. But others, including Wuer Kaixi laid the blame at the students' feet. They had refused to let the delegates stick to the agenda and then had disrupted the meeting altogether by rushing the building. "The talks were wrecked by the students themselves. I felt that May 14 was a big setback for the student movement."

After the failed meeting, intellectuals and student leaders worried about what to do next. Gorbachev was arriving the next day, and they were afraid that the government would decide to clear the square by force that night. A group of twelve intellectuals—some of the country's most famous writers and scholars—decided to go to the square and speak directly to the hunger strikers. The twelve pleaded with the strikers and their supporters to show the government they could be rational and reasonable by temporarily vacating the square for Gorbachev's visit. The hunger strikers refused.

■ GORBACHEV ARRIVES

The strikers' refusal to move was troubling to intellectuals who supported the movement and to the more moderate factions within the movement. With Chai Ling in charge, the hunger strikers were ignoring elected student leadership—the movement's link to the government. They established their own union, the Tiananmen Square Hunger Strike Headquarters.

The strikers had announced a willingness to die at Tiananmen. But movement moderates worried that the government would call the strikers' bluff and let students starve to death. Or it would claim

Chai Ling speaks to thousands of students in Tiananmen Square in May 1989. She was the leader of the hunger strike.

that it had exhausted all good faith efforts and use that as an excuse to crush the movement. Rumors began to circulate that Deng intended to declare martial law in Beijing—an emergency measure in which the government allows the military to take over policing an area and maintaining civil order.

Yet support for the hunger strikers grew. Thousands of students were arriving from other Chinese cities and joining the strike. The number of hunger strikers grew to about thirty-one hundred. Supporters numbered about three hundred thousand.

Beijing workers and other residents donated money and supplies. The Red Cross and Beijing emergency services were on hand to offer treatment. It did not take long for the lack of food to seriously affect

Medics rush an ill student from the hunger strike in Tiananmen Square to a hospital on May 16, 1989.

already exhausted students. Within the first couple of days, medical teams were giving intravenous glucose (blood sugar) and taking fainting or feverish hunger strikers to the hospital. Medical workers also warned that sanitation conditions on the square would quickly become a problem, and any infectious disease could easily spread through the crowds. As Beijing residents watched the students weakly drinking water or shivering under blankets in midday, their anger at the government grew.

When Gorbachev arrived in Beijing at noon on May 15, PRC president Yang Shangkun met him and his aides at the airport. The motorcade was taken into central Beijing not by the normal ceremonial route but by one of the city's secondary roads. The Russian visitors were whisked into government buildings to begin their round of meetings.

Meanwhile, many of the reporters and photographers sent to Beijing to record Gorbachev's arrival were on Tiananmen Square interviewing students. At one in the afternoon, the strike headquarters held a press conference on the square. Chai Ling announced that if the government continued to ignore the strikers, they would self-immolate (commit suicide by setting themselves on fire). Word spread that some students had made out their wills and purchased gasoline.

President Yang met with Gorbachev on May 15 inside the Great Hall of the People. He told Gorbachev that the student movement was part of China's reform and that during any time of great change, mistakes would be made. But he expressed confidence that the student crisis could be solved peacefully. The next day, Deng Xiaoping and Zhao Ziyang met with the Russian leader. At his meeting, Zhao repeated

Deng Xiaoping *(right)* shakes hands with Russian leader Mikhail Gorbachev in Beijing on May 16, 1989.

Yang's sentiments. He also explained in passing that Deng, although retired, still held enormous influence in the party and that most Politburo decisions passed through Deng.

Late in the afternoon, Yan Mingfu went to Tiananmen Square to plead personally with the hunger strikers. He asked them not to endanger their health but to return to classes. The strikers told him that they would not stop until the government met their demands. Yan then offered himself as a hostage. If the students ended the hunger strike, they could keep him in their custody until the government responded to them. The strikers admired Yan's sincerity, but they refused.

▪ ZHAO'S DOWNFALL

Yan reported the outcome of his efforts to Zhao, and Zhao called an emergency meeting of the Politburo. Zhao's frustration was clear. He told Politburo comrades that the old student leadership was fragmented and that newcomers to the square were excited and unfocused. "If we don't get a handle on this thing quickly," he reportedly said, "if we just let it keep going, we could see a real nightmare."

Li Peng repeated his position that the movement's goal was to bring down the Communist government, and Politburo hard-liners agreed. Zhao suggested once again that they revise the April 26 editorial, and once again, the hard-liners refused. The meeting ended.

May 17, the fifth day of the hunger strike, saw the largest demonstration in the history of the People's Republic. Almost two million people marched through Beijing. Factory workers, teachers, students, government workers, and even army officers demonstrated in support of the hunger strikers. The protesters called for Deng to give up his influence over the Politburo and for Li Peng to resign. In twenty other Chinese cities, hundreds of thousands of people also demonstrated in support of the Beijing students.

As demonstrators filled the streets, the Politburo took their impasse (failure to agree) to Deng at his home. Deng's vote often operated as a tiebreaker in the reform-versus-hard-liner Politburo. This time, Deng voted with Li Peng's faction. Li Peng saw his opportunity and struck.

Almost two million people gathered in Tiananmen Square on May 17, 1989, to support the Beijing students and their cause.

He blamed Zhao for allowing the student movement to escalate instead of ending it in April. Further, Li said, Zhao had contradicted Deng's own position—clearly stated in the April 26 editorial—at the Asian Development Bank meeting. And, Li asked, why did Zhao tell Gorbachev about Deng's position within the Politburo? Li cast that remark as an attempt by Zhao to discredit Deng. If all final decisions rested with Deng, was Zhao trying to say that Deng was ultimately responsible for the current crisis?

Zhao tried to defend himself, but Deng sided with Li. Seeing that, other Politburo members who had stayed silent or were on the fence began to agree with Li. With the impasse broken, Deng announced his solution for solving the student crisis: "After thinking long and hard about this, I've concluded that we should bring in the People's Liberation Army and declare martial law in Beijing."

Zhao accepted that the majority of the Politburo agreed with the decision. But he immediately made it clear that he would have personal difficulty enforcing the decision to impose martial law. The meeting

MARTIAL LAW

Most countries have some provision for instituting martial law. Countries commonly use a form of martial law during natural disasters when a government declares a state of emergency. Under those circumstances, military troops can, for example, enforce curfews and arrest looters to maintain civil order. In China, under martial law, students and other citizens cannot attend public protests and rallies, circulate petitions, boycott classes, or call work strikes. During martial law, Chinese citizens can also be prevented from leaving the country, and foreign journalists can be prevented from entering China.

broke for a few hours and resumed in the evening. At that point, Zhao offered his resignation to Yang Shangkun, saying that health problems would prevent him from serving any further. Yang would not accept the resignation, but Zhao's political career was effectively over. He attended one last Politburo meeting on May 18.

Very early the next morning, at four, Li Peng and Zhao both visited the student hunger strikers at Tiananmen. Zhao sadly told students that he was old and did not matter anymore but that they should think of their youth and health. He begged them to end the strike. The students were moved—some to tears—but they refused. Soon after, Li reported Zhao's emotional plea to Yang Shangkun, who told Deng. Deng was furious and accused Zhao of trying to win student sympathy. Zhao was labeled undisciplined and uncooperative. As Deng fumed over Zhao and Tiananmen Square filled once again with demonstrators, Li Peng was invited to move into Deng's former quarters at Zhongnanhai. What the intellectuals had warned the students of had come to pass: the hard-liners were in power.

CHAPTER 5

DEADLOCK

"Tiananmen Square has become
a symbol of democracy in China.
We can't abandon it."

–Chen Di, a student from Shenyang, China,
on the protesters' determination to remain on the square, May 30, 1989

On May 19, the leadership of the People's Liberation Army sent notices to military units around the country that martial law would be declared in Beijing. Military officers were to begin moving the troops. Because the troops might be clashing with Chinese citizens, preparation would have to include political thought work. There was evidence that the many officers, even high-ranking ones, did not agree with the government's position. Some agreed with the students, and some thought the government was overreacting. The military had to fix that situation as the troops rolled out to enforce martial law. The military declared that officers and soldiers had to understand the importance of the April 26 editorial and agree that the student movement was a threat to national stability.

In Beijing a new development added to the government's concern. Local factory employees had begun gathering on Chang'an Boulevard in front of Tiananmen. They declared their intention to form an Autonomous Federation of Workers. Like official student organizations, all workers' unions had to be approved and overseen by the CCP. The federation would be independent and run by workers. The federation threatened to call a twenty-four-hour work strike in support of the student movement. Such strikes, if they spread, could cripple China's economy and cause far more harm than the student protests. The federation's threat was, as Stanford University (California) professor Andrew Walder said, a "severe popular challenge to Communist Party rule."

RUMORS

The situation in Beijing was growing more chaotic. On the square, the number of hunger strike supporters dipped. New rules kept many out of the square. Anyone entering the area had to have an official pass.

But even as the number of Beijing demonstrators dwindled, more students continued to arrive from other cities. Government reports estimated that more than fifty thousand students arrived by train in the three days preceding May 19. More arrived by bus and car. At first the newcomers, who were refused entry to the square, camped out on the street. But gradually, they replaced the Beijing students who had left the square exhausted or discouraged. By the third week of May, almost 70 percent of the students on the square were from outside Beijing.

Leadership among the students grew increasingly confusing. Rival groups set up their own loudspeaker equipment, and their broadcasts drowned out one another. Student leaders argued and even physically fought. Rumors began to spread. Some people claimed, for example, that Wang Dan was only faking his hunger strike, that he was secretly sneaking off to eat whenever he got hungry. His defenders claimed that government agents were starting such rumors to discredit the students. But the rumors still circulated, especially among newcomers, who did not know the Beijing student leaders.

In the late afternoon of May 19, a more serious rumor reached Tiananmen Square. The students heard that the government had agreed to declare martial law. They also heard that Zhao Ziyang had been fired.

NEW **LEADERSHIP**

Li Peng managed to prevail in his battle with Zhao Ziyang. But Zhao's ouster did not turn out to be the career triumph Li might have expected. On May 21, 1989, the Politburo elders met to discuss Zhao's replacement. Li's name did not come up. He was too deeply unpopular with the Chinese people to be considered for the post of party general secretary. Instead, party elders focused on Jiang Zemin. As party secretary in Shanghai, Jiang was successful in controlling demonstrations in that city. He was considered highly intelligent and a tried-and-true party member. On May 27, the elders appointed Jiang as CCP general secretary.

Later that evening, Li Peng addressed military leaders. His address was nationally broadcast, and the students, as well as everyone else in China, learned that the rumor about martial law was true.

The students reacted angrily to the news about Zhao and to Li's speech. They took to the streets to demonstrate, chanting against a government led by old men. They also specifically criticized Deng, seeing his hand in Zhao's downfall. They called him a dictator and demanded his resignation. Students were angry, but they were also frightened by the news about martial law. The army had moved in to the outskirts of Beijing and was awaiting orders.

■ A SHORT-LIVED COMPROMISE

The Beijing city government had sent buses to the square to shelter students during spring thunderstorms. But the students suspected that the buses were a plot. They believed that once they climbed inside, they would be driven away. So they threw the bus drivers out of the vehicles, punctured the tires, and removed steering wheels. After securing the buses, student leaders took turns sleeping inside. It was outside one of these buses that student leaders gathered on the evening of May 19. Chai Ling, Feng Congde, Shen Tong, Wang Dan, Wuer Kaixi, and others met to discuss their next step. At the same time, Zhang Boli held a meeting and a vote on another bus. Both groups agreed to end the hunger strike. They believed that in doing so, they would remove the government's justification for declaring martial law.

At about nine in the evening, Chai Ling called a press conference. She announced to Chinese and foreign reporters that the hunger strike was over. In its place, students would stage a peaceful mass sit-in. Students in the crowd immediately accused her of selling out. Even her own husband, Feng Congde, declared that the student leaders were not in a position to make that decision. Feng called for a second vote. This time, students on the square voted to continue the hunger strike. Shortly after Chai's press conference, the official loudspeakers on Tiananmen Square crackled on. Beijing mayor Yang Shangkun announced that the government had no choice but to bring troops into the city to restore order.

LONG LIVE THE PLA

The next day, May 20, the government formally declared martial law. Army troops in tanks and armored personnel carriers (APCs) began moving from Beijing's vast suburbs toward the city. These troops numbered more than twenty-five hundred, including officers. About five thousand local soldiers were garrisoned (stationed) at the Great Hall of the People. Citizens were notified that they should stay off the streets as the army moved in. But thousands of Beijing residents ignored the orders. Demonstrators again filled the streets.

On May 21, students at Tiananmen organized a new group, Defend Tiananmen Square Headquarters. Chai Ling was chosen as the headquarters' commander, and Zhang Boli and Li Lu (a graduate student at Nanjing University) were named deputies. The group was strongly

Citizens surround a truck trying to transport army troops into the city center of Beijing on May 20, 1989.

supported by the newcomers (the students from outside Beijing) and almost unanimously in favor of continuing the hunger strike. Other student leaders such as Shen Tong, Wang Dan, and Wuer Kaixi felt that the hunger strikers were indulging in an emotional gesture, rather than making rational decisions. But they felt that their voices were increasingly drowned out by the enthusiastic newcomers. On May 22, Wuer was expelled from the square after making a speech asking students to retreat.

Among Beijing residents, rumors began circulating about the troops. Many of the rumors were sympathetic to the common soldiers. Some said that soldiers had not really been told why they were in Beijing. They had been prevented from reading any newspapers or listening to TV or radio for weeks. Other rumors suggested that some very young soldiers from rural areas did not even realize that they were in Beijing. Demonstrators began chanting, "Long live the PLA" and "The people love the people's army." Residents offered the troops food, water, and flowers. But they also firmly blocked the troops' movements. They set up roadblocks with "steel dividers that resembled bicycle racks and anything else they could find."

Students offer food to soldiers headed for Tiananmen Square on May 21, 1989. The students' offering of goodwill also served as a roadblock to the vehicles.

Unwilling to use any force at that point, the troops withdrew. By May 23, most of the tanks and APCs had pulled back to the outskirts of Beijing. But stories flew that soldiers wearing street clothes were sneaking into the city on subway trains. Residents began setting up checkpoints at subway stations or simply blocking off the station entrances. In some stations, subway workers turned off the power, stranding the trains.

In many places, withdrawing troops had left behind trucks full of helmets and weapons. Most likely, the gear was intended for the soldiers who had snuck into the city in street clothes. But residents jumped to the conclusion that the abandoned equipment was a trick. The army, rumors said, hoped that students would raid the trucks and arm themselves, thus giving the soldiers a reason to use force.

In the United States, Great Britain, and other Western countries, Chinese students wrote letters and gathered petitions to send to the Chinese government. Western governments also watched the martial law situation with concern. U.S. president George H. W. Bush urged Chinese leaders to show restraint and find a peaceful solution. European leaders suggested that China's actions at this point could affect its trade and investment opportunities.

■■■■ ■ THE THREAT OF FORCE

On the square, students heard rumors that government—now completely controlled by hard-liners—was no longer interested in compromise. They heard that Yang Shangkun intended to bring troops all the way into Tiananmen Square no matter what the students did. The troops, it was said, would not fire on anyone. But they would clear the square. Students also heard rumors that Li Peng was releasing Beijing prisoners, emptying the jails in preparation for the mass arrest of students.

Some accounts suggest that Mayor Yang and the government hoped that the mere presence of the troops and the threat of arrests would be enough to get the students off the square. But in fact, the students were heartened by Beijing residents' reaction to martial law. They felt reassured that they still had the support of the people. Workers were again threatening a general strike. Chinese writers and scholars had organized as the Association of Beijing Intellectuals. The association was growing more vocal in its opposition to Li Peng and government hard-liners. Students also heard rumors that the military was deeply divided over martial law. Eight PLA generals had written a letter to the Central Military Commission requesting that martial law end and that the troops leave Beijing. Students on the square began to relax a little. They read, studied, and listened to music on portable stereos. Around Beijing, residents relaxed too. No demonstrations occurred.

Student leadership, however, remained divided. On May 27, a student group called the Alliance to Protect the Constitution voted to recommend that students end their occupation of Tiananmen Square by

Students on Tiananmen Square relax during an impromptu concert on May 25, 1989.

May 30. They announced their recommendation at a press conference. The very next day, Defend Tiananmen Square Headquarters held their own vote. The voters, mostly non-Beijing students, rejected the alliance's decision and announced their intention to stay on the square.

Feeling caught between Beijing student organizations and outside students, Chai Ling, Wang Dan, and other student leaders resigned on May 29. After the resignations, students in the square formed the All-China Autonomous Students Federation. This umbrella group would represent student organizations from around the country, not just from Beijing. The group voted to stay on the square until the National People's Congress met on June 20.

"FOR FREEDOM"

Residents in Hong Kong were deeply concerned over the unfolding events in Tiananmen Square. Hong Kong was a Chinese territory long under the control of the British government. The territory was due to be returned to the People's Republic of China in 1997, and Hong Kong residents worried that hard-line Communists were gaining power in the PRC government.

On Saturday, May 27, 1989, a group of artists in Hong Kong hosted a twelve-hour "Concert for Democracy in China." The concert's theme song, "For Freedom," was performed by Hong Kong singer Lu Kuan-Tin. Other famous Hong Kong musicians and TV stars also performed. About 300,000 people attended, and the concert raised more than HK$12 million in support of the student movement. The next day, more than 1.5 million Hong Kong residents marched through the city in support of the Beijing students.

■ THE GODDESS OF DEMOCRACY

For several days, students at the Central Academy of Fine Arts in Beijing had been working on a project. They intended the work to be a symbol of the student movement and something that would mark the movement as part of the long tradition of civil rights struggles around the world. On the evening of May 29, academy students rolled the pieces of their large project through the streets of Beijing. When they reached Tiananmen, they began assembling the framework.

The next day, their work was unveiled to a crowd of tens of thousands. It was a 33-foot-tall (10 m) statue called the Goddess of Democracy. The plaster statue wore a flowing gown and held up a lighted torch.

Protesters in Hong Kong march in support of those in Tiananmen Square on May 28, 1989.

Students surround the Goddess of Democracy on May 30, 1989. Behind them is the Mao Zedong portrait that hangs in Tiananmen Square.

The resemblance to the Statue of Liberty in the United States was seen as both an appeal to people in the West and a jab at the anti-Western Chinese government. The statue faced the portrait of Chairman Mao across Tiananmen Square.

As students celebrated the unveiling of the statue, more news reached the square. Beijing police had arrested leaders of the Autonomous Federation of Workers. Also detained were eleven members of the Flying Tigers, a group of volunteers who helped spread movement news throughout Beijing. More than four hundred workers and students left the square for the headquarters of the Beijing Public Security Bureau (the offices responsible for city policing and public order). There they staged a sit-in demanding the release of the arrested leaders.

On May 31, Beida student Guo Haifeng led a reorganization of the square. Thousands of students had been on the square for more than six weeks. The tents were tattered, and garbage was piled up. Hong Kong supporters had donated new tents. Students began tearing down the old tents and picking up the garbage. Beijing sanitation workers moved through with spray trucks, washing down the pavement. The square was busy but quiet.

Workers attempt to clean up Tiananmen Square on May 28, 1989. A few days later, students organized to help with the cleanup.

Elsewhere in Beijing that day, however, the streets rattled with military jeep patrols. In the suburbs, police organized pro-government demonstrations. Thousands of party workers and residents marched through the streets chanting slogans against Fang Lizhi and other pro-democracy radicals.

At about five in the evening, leaders of the Autonomous Federation of Workers were released from police custody. But their supporters did not realize this. About three thousand students marched to Tiananmen Square to again protest the leaders' arrests. More students and workers protested later that evening in front of the public security headquarters. The protests moved to Xinhua Gate, where students shouted slogans against Li Peng. Beijing police let the protesters remain, but they pushed away foreign reporters and photographers. The next day, the government banned all foreign news coverage of Beijing demonstrations.

ANOTHER HUNGER STRIKE

Some protests continued on the streets. But on the square, the movement was losing steam again. Many Beijing students were returning to classes. Student leaders focused on their own power struggles, while remaining students seemed to be simply waiting to see what would happen next.

Writer Liu Xiaobo felt that this combination of infighting at the top and passivity among the ranks would kill the movement. The situation, he felt, reflected the mistakes of Chinese history and not the spirit of a civil rights struggle. Liu decided to make his own sacrifice to spur the movement on again. On June 2, he announced that he would go on a hunger strike at the heroes' monument. Popular singer Hou Dejian, editor Gao Xin, and businessman Zhou Tuo joined him. The four hunger strikers made speeches, and Hou sang. "Chinese democracy," the hunger strikers declared, "must be built on the basis of tolerance and cooperation. . . . We call upon every citizen from the government level to the grassroots to abandon the old political culture." Their words inspired the students, and crowds of Beijing residents began returning to the square.

Activists on the square refocused themselves on the spirit of the movement. But behind the scenes, the government was stepping up its rhetoric as well. Deng, the other elders, and the Politburo continued to rail at the black hands behind the movement. They turned particular attention on foreign influences. At a June 2 meeting with the elders and the Politburo Standing Committee, Deng reportedly said:

> The Western world, especially the United States, has thrown its entire propaganda machine into agitation work and has given a lot of encouragement and assistance to the so-called democrats or opposition in China—the people who are in fact the scum of the Chinese nation.

Both sides of the Beijing confrontation had been playing a waiting game. But the threat of martial law hadn't been enough, and the government was under increasing pressure to get the city under control. Embassy officials, reporters, and some student leaders noted ominous signs. Tens of thousands of troops were massed in the near suburbs. Military jeeps were patrolling the streets. Foreign media were being banned. Foreign workers and students were being advised to prepare for evacuation from the city. Then, on the night of June 2, the order came. Yang Shangkun told troops to begin moving into city center. The military also took control of all major media.

CHAPTER 6

THE
TROOPS
ARRIVE

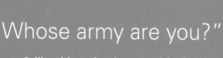

Whose army are you?"

—Beijing citizens shouting at People's Liberation Army
soldiers as martial law was enforced, June 3, 1989

Most of the ten thousand to fifteen thousand troops had been waiting on the west side of the city, about 3 to 4 miles (5 to 6 kilometers) from Tiananmen. But troops were massed on streets to the north, south, and east too. After midnight on Saturday, June 3, tanks and APCs full of soldiers began moving toward the city center. Soldiers were ordered not to fire on citizens. But they were helmeted and armed with automatic weapons. They had been told to reclaim Tiananmen Square at any cost.

As they had before, Beijing residents managed to stop troop movements in many areas. Residents pulled city buses and dump trucks across streets to serve as barricades. On some streets, soldiers left behind vehicles after being surrounded by citizens. Citizens found machine guns, rifles, grenades, and gas masks inside the vehicles. People displayed the gear as proof that the government had ordered the military to use deadly force. Then, wary of being caught with weapons, the citizens turned everything over to the police.

Beijing residents block soldiers from moving toward Tiananmen Square in the days before June 4, 1989.

Midafternoon, near the west gate of the Great Hall, the troops that had been garrisoned in the Great Hall ran into a large crowd. The two groups faced each other in a standoff for more than two hours. U.S. State Department telegrams noted that many citizens "sternly lectured" very young soldiers about how wrong it was to march against their own people. Some elderly women reportedly called the soldiers "a disgrace to the PLA." Finally, the troops returned to the Great Hall, overwhelmed by the size of the crowd. But other troops continued to move into the city.

Soldiers attempt to force their way past citizens outside the Great Hall of the People on June 3, 1989.

BLOODY CONFLICT

Over the course of the day, soldiers and citizens grew angrier and more emotional. Confrontations escalated. Many of the troops traveled along Chang'an Boulevard, and several incidents occurred at major intersections along that route. At the Muxidi, Liubukuo, and Xidan intersections, citizens blocked military trucks and surrounded small groups of soldiers who were on foot. Some threw Molotov cocktails (bottles filled with fuel and lit with rag fuses) at APCs and tanks. Some soldiers reported that they were fired on by unknown rooftop gunmen. After military vehicles were abandoned, citizens set them on fire.

Soldiers threw tear gas into the crowds. The explosions of the tear gas canisters injured many people, including children. At Zhongnanhai, troops used billy clubs (heavy wooden sticks) to drive off protesters. Reports from witnesses and foreign embassies said that hospitals were already filling up with wounded people.

Radio and TV stations began broadcasting emergency orders. The orders warned people to return to their homes and announced that the military would not tolerate violations of martial law. The broadcasts had little effect on citizens.

By evening, troops had reached inner Beijing. On Chang'an Boulevard just outside the Forbidden City, an APC became separated from other military vehicles. Trying to return quickly to the ranks, the vehicle ran over several protesters. A crowd surrounded the APC and pulled out its crew. In view of other troops, the crowd killed the soldiers and set the APC on fire.

Protesters stop a burning APC near Tiananmen Square on June 4, 1989.

As more heavily armed troops moved into central Beijing on June 3, 1989, they began firing into crowds of citizens on the street. Outraged at seeing this, people in nearby buildings threw dishes and pots down on the troops. In response, troops sprayed the buildings with gunfire. "Several people died in their homes that night," Canadian reporter Jan Wong recalled. "The nephew of the chief justice of the supreme court of China was shot in his own kitchen." Troops also fired on hotels where they knew foreign reporters and photographers were staying.

At about ten at night, just after the third emergency broadcast, troops began firing guns into crowds. They also fired into groups of bystanders who were not taking part in the protests. People tried to carry gunshot wound victims to hospitals, but many lay in the street where they fell.

■ SURROUNDED

By about one in the morning on Sunday, June 4, troops had surrounded Tiananmen Square. They took positions on the steps of the Great Hall and the China National Museum on either side of the square. The soldiers waited for orders, while student leaders frantically tried to move protesters back to the heroes' monument.

About three thousand protesters remained on the square. Many did not know what was happening on the streets of Beijing. They could hear gunfire, and they knew many soldiers were nearby. But the protesters believed that if they practiced passive resistance—refusing to move or fight—the soldiers would try to clear the square with billy clubs or nonlethal rubber bullets. About two o'clock, students who had been on the streets arrived with the news that the troops were firing real bullets at crowds.

Writer Liu Xiaobo and the other three hunger strikers discussed this news among themselves. They felt that remaining on the square was too much of a gamble. They decided to try to negotiate with the soldiers waiting on Chang'an Boulevard. The hunger strikers would convince the students to leave the square if the soldiers promised to let everyone go unharmed. At about four o'clock, the four hunger strikers found some military officers. As they approached, soldiers drew their guns. The singer Hou Dejian held up his white vest as a sign of surrender. The officers listened to the strikers' offer and accepted. But the officers gave three thousand protesters only a half hour to clear the square.

The hunger strikers returned to the heroes' monument with their news. Some students were angry that the four had talked to the military. They called Liu Xiaobo and the others traitors. But student leaders decided to take a vote on the next action. It was a close vote, but Feng Congde announced the result in favor of immediately vacating the square. They would all leave through the southeast corner.

■ CLEARING THE SQUARE

At about five o'clock, student leaders stood together for a few minutes deciding how to proceed. Feng Congde said, "They left only a small gap for us to leave. . . . Nobody dared move at first." But students soon began forming lines to file out. As they did, troops entered the square with guns drawn. "The soldiers came right up in front of us," student Liang Xiaoyan recalled. "They were in full battle gear." Some soldiers pushed their way to the monument, beating students who stood in the way. At the monument, the soldiers set up machine guns. Tanks also rolled into the square. The tanks crushed the Goddess of Democracy statue. They also rolled over tents, even as witnesses screamed that some tents were still occupied.

Part of the mass of students thought that heading toward the China National Museum would be the easiest way out. But as they approached, they were blocked by soldiers. The soldiers pushed them back. Students who resisted or argued were beaten or shot. At gunpoint, the students were pushed out of the square at the southeast corner, near Qianmen.

Outside the square, some students ran for the nearby railway station. Others began to walk back toward their campuses along West Chang'an Boulevard. As a group approached the Liubukou intersection, they heard a loud noise behind them. Suddenly, Zhang Boli recalled, "a speeding tank came upon us like a gust of wind

Tanks roll through Tiananmen Square the morning of June 4, 1989.

trying to cut through the lines of people." Twenty-two-year-old student Fang Zheng was also at the scene: "In the blink of an eye, the tank was approaching the sidewalk and closing in on me. It seemed as if the barrel of its gun was inches from my face. I could not dodge it in time. I threw myself to the ground and began to roll. But it was too late." Fang's upper body landed between the tank's treads. But his legs were run over and crushed.

More tanks followed and ran people down. Tank crews shot and fired tear gas at the crowds. Throughout the day, soldiers continued to drive people away from the square. They fired on crowds. They beat reporters and photographers and smashed their cameras. Citizens continued to fight back, clashing with soldiers (and in several incidents, killing soldiers) and setting fire to hundreds of military vehicles. But with the square cleared, the Chinese government declared victory. It had, it announced, saved Beijing from the "small handful of rioters" who had stirred up so much trouble.

CHAPTER 7

REACTION

"I deeply deplore the decision to use force against peaceful demonstrators and the consequent loss of life. We urged and continue to urge nonviolence, restraint, and dialogue. Tragically, another course has been chosen."

–U.S. president George H. W. Bush, in reaction to the
June 4 clearing of Tiananmen Square, 1989

Beginning on June 4, tens of thousands of students in Shanghai, Changchun, Nanjing, and several other Chinese cities marched to protest the deaths in Beijing. They blocked railroad tracks, highways, and bridges. Many distributed leaflets with the latest news from the capital.

People in Hong Kong, Taiwan, and Macau (a Chinese territory) held memorial services, vigils, and rallies for those killed in Beijing. They laid wreaths and flowers and raised money to help survivors. In Canada, Europe, Japan, Mexico, and the United States, people also gathered to remember the dead and condemn the Chinese government. The rallies were especially strong and emotional in cities with large Chinese student and immigrant populations. Chinese overseas were outraged and grieved by news photos of bloodied protesters, terrified citizens, and warlike chaos on the streets of the capital. Thousands called for the current Chinese leadership to step down. Hundreds of Chinese students overseas resigned from the Communist Youth League and the CCP.

On June 5, government leaders from Australia, Europe, Japan, South Korea, and the United States commented on the military action at Tiananmen Square. President Bush condemned the crackdown. He announced that the United States would halt exports and the sale of any military equipment to China. He suspended relations between U.S. and Chinese military leaders. Margaret Thatcher, the prime minister of the United Kingdom, said she was "shocked and appalled by the shootings." French foreign minister Roland Dumas called the military action "a bloody repression." The World Bank, an international financial group, suspended monetary loans to China. Many countries announced that they would allow Chinese students to extend their stays in those countries. In response, the Chinese government said that other countries should not interfere in China's affairs.

PICKING UP THE PIECES

After Tiananmen Square was cleared, most students made their way back to their campuses. There, student leaders called on people to stand up and tell the truth about the military action. They called on workers to strike and boycott businesses.

But the student leaders knew they could not stay where they were for long. Security forces were already on campus searching for them. Zhang Boli and his wife escaped from Beijing on bicycles, dodging

TANK MAN

On June 5, 1989, a column of military tanks rolled down Chang'an Boulevard near Tiananmen Square. Suddenly, a young man stepped off the curb and stopped directly in the tanks' path. He was unarmed, wore a light shirt, and carried a shopping bag. Reporter Jan Wong was watching from her hotel balcony. "I held my breath," she recalled. "I was convinced he was going to die. My eyes filled with tears."

But instead of running over the man, the first tank in the column shuddered to a halt. Its front end was only a few feet from the man. When he refused to move, the tank attempted to go around him. But the man again jumped in its path. Then he climbed onto the tank and pounded on its hatch door. Witnesses reported that the young man shouted something at the tank crew. He then jumped down and stood in front of the tank again until three bystanders ran up and hustled him away.

Foreign photographers watching Chang'an Boulevard from nearby hotels snapped photos of the scene (right). In the days before cell phone cameras, the film had to be smuggled out of the hotel past security police. But soon the image appeared in newspapers and on TV around the world. It became one of the most famous photos of the twentieth century. The young man came to stand as a symbol of the power of individual courage.

military vehicles and stopping at friends' houses to gather money. Shen Tong hid at his parents' Beijing home and then at an abandoned building while waiting for his travel visa to the United States to be finalized. Wang Dan, Feng Congde, and Chai Ling made plans to escape the country through Hong Kong. Fang Lizhi and Li Shuxian sought

No one knew the man's name or who he was. Some human rights workers identified him as a nineteen-year-old Beijing resident, Wang Weilin. But that information was not confirmed. News sources began calling him the Unknown Rebel and Tank Man. Some journalists believe that the people who hustled Tank Man off the boulevard were probably security forces. They believe that the man was subsequently jailed or probably executed. Others are more hopeful. They argue that if security had caught Tank Man, they would have shown him in public—either to prove that they had not executed him or to make an example of him. These journalists believe that Tank Man slipped back into anonymity and may still live in Beijing.

asylum (protection from political persecution) at the U.S. Embassy in Beijing until they could escape from China.

The streets of Beijing were fairly empty, except for military patrols. People stayed in their houses, and shops and restaurants were closed. But one group persisted in showing up at Tiananmen Square—the parents of missing college students. Parents also went to the universities and hospitals to look for the missing. At the square, soldiers drove the parents away. But they kept returning, insisting that they only wanted news about their children.

At this time, reports began circulating that military groups were fighting with one another. Many people blamed most of the violence during the crackdown on the 27th and 38th armies (divisions of the PLA). Rumors swirled that these two armies were fighting with other divisions and with armed police units.

■ ■ ■ DIPLOMATIC INCIDENTS

In light of the continued instability, foreign embassies in Beijing began urging their citizens on June 6 to leave China. Many tourists, visiting professors, and diplomatic workers were anxious to leave. Some had been in the square and on the streets and had witnessed the violence. But even those who had stayed in their houses and apartments were frightened by the frequent gunfire and explosions. "There was talk about the army splitting," U.S. educator Gary Pranger recalled. Pranger taught Chinese students at a diplomatic school about 2 miles (3 km) west of Tiananmen Square. "If there was going to be a battle [between rival armies], it was going to be in our neighborhood."

Pranger, his wife, and their two young children lived in a housing unit with other American, British, French, and Russian teachers. At about eleven in the morning on June 6, U.S. Embassy workers arrived and advised the American teachers to pack what they could carry. The Prangers were moved to a hotel on Chang'an Boulevard while they waited for their June 9 airplane reservations. But sensing growing tension in the city, they decided to go to the airport early on June 7. They arrived to find chaos. The airport was staffed for normal business

A tour bus leaving Beijing passes through throngs of Chinese citizens surrounding a victim of June 4 violence.

but packed with the sudden influx of people. Travelers clamored for any available tickets to Taiwan or Japan. Pranger believes that sympathy for his children and other young children waiting to fly out convinced airport personnel to open up more ticket gates and begin arranging for more flights. "The Chinese people love children," Pranger observed.

Later that day, PLA troops fired into the Jianguomenwai Diplomatic Compound on East Chang'an Boulevard. The compound was home for many foreign diplomats and journalists in Beijing and included the U.S. Embassy. The PLA claimed that they had been fired on first by snipers (hidden gunmen) inside the compound. But U.S. officials countered that the shooting was in retaliation for harboring Fang Lizhi and Li Shuxian.

Soldiers with machine guns surrounded another nearby diplomatic compound, refusing to let anyone in or out. According to some reports, they had stopped clearly marked diplomatic cars on Beijing streets and robbed the occupants. After these incidents, the United States and several other governments ordered the evacuation from Beijing of all nonessential embassy personnel and their families.

■ COUNTING THE DEAD

As the Chinese government worked to regain control of the city, they began to release figures on the numbers of people killed and wounded. Hospitals and morgues were ordered not to give out figures to the media or aid organizations. The CCP wanted to control the information. At a June 7 press conference, government official Yuan Mu announced that about seven thousand people were wounded during the crackdown. Five thousand of them were soldiers. Yuan also claimed that of the three hundred who died, twenty-three were soldiers and thirty-six were students. The rest were citizens, mostly violent rioters and "hoodlums." Aid and human rights organizations such as the Chinese Red Cross and Amnesty International immediately contradicted that report. They claimed that the Chinese government was greatly underestimating civilian injuries and deaths.

On June 8, Li Peng appeared in public for the first time since the crackdown. He attended a reception for the military to congratulate the troops. Li praised the bravery and self-control soldiers exhibited while facing down violent rioters and antigovernment counterrevolutionaries. The speech was broadcast nationally on CCTV.

6/4

In the West, the 1989 Beijing protests are often referred to as the Tiananmen Square protests or even simply "Tiananmen Square." But many protests and demonstrations took place in Tiananmen Square during the twentieth century. So in China, the 1989 protests are usually called the June 4 demonstrations. Often that is abbreviated as 6/4.

The next day, June 9, Deng Xiaoping made his first public appearance since May 16. On national TV, he too praised the bravery and restraint of the troops. He called for a moment of silence in memory of the soldiers killed. These "deceased martyrs," Deng said, had prevented the overthrow of the government by counterrevolutionary forces supported by the West. With the storm over, he said, China was now free to continue on her path of reform.

■ WANTED

By June 11, the military was securely in control of the city and arrests began. Beijing authorities took more than four hundred people, including student and labor leaders, into custody. The Chinese government issued an arrest warrant for Fang Lizhi and Li Shuxian on June 11. They were charged with spreading antigovernment propaganda and instigating counterrevolutionary activities. The government distributed

PLA troops guard the Gate of Heavenly Peace following the eviction of the protesters from Tiananmen Square in June 1989.

wanted posters of the couple around Beijing, and Chinese newspaper articles criticized the couple as traitors. CCTV aired on-the-street-style interviews of Beijing citizens saying that the fact that the couple had run to the U.S. Embassy for protection proved they were Western-backed counterrevolutionaries.

To further bolster their control of Beijing, police and soldiers were given permission to shoot rioters, counterrevolutionaries, and "people gathering together to cause chaos." The government banned all autonomous student and labor organizations on June 12. It demanded that leaders of such groups turn themselves in. Anyone caught assisting the leaders would be arrested. In fact, the government urged, "every citizen should search for criminals and report them." Telephone hotlines were set up to assist citizens in reporting counterrevolutionary activities.

On June 13, the government issued a most wanted list for twenty-one student leaders. The list included names, descriptions, and photographs and was broadcast on national TV. Zhang Boli, in hiding in northern China, watched the broadcast. Next to him at the dining table, a friend grasped his hand and hoped that security police did not have Zhang's name. "But they did," Zhang said. "There I was at Tiananmen Square, wearing a sunhat, holding a bullhorn, speaking to the audience." Wang Dan, Wuer Kaixi, Chai Ling, Feng Congde, Zhou Yongjun, and Guo Haifeng were also on the list. Wang Dan topped the list. He heard the news on the radio in a ship's barbershop, as he fled the country. "I was totally numb," he said, "not angry and not afraid."

> "I had prepared to die, and imagined that even as I faced rifle fire, I would still feel calm inside, since I had done nothing to regret. . . . Afterwards, however, I still felt a heavy burden of guilt about the citizens and students who had fallen, because I should have been the first to fall."
>
> —*Wang Dan, recalling June 4, 1989, in his 1998 book* Prison Memoirs

Immediately after the June 4 crackdown, twenty-year-old history student Wang Dan got on a ship headed for the Chinese city of Nanjing. He planned to escape China. After about a month, he decided to return to Beijing. "I was exhausted. I'd been all around the south of China, but I'd had enough. I decided I'd rather be arrested than on the run like that," he later told reporters. Wang was arrested in July 1989 for spreading counterrevolutionary propaganda and sentenced to four years in prison. During that time, he spent months in solitary confinement in a 16-foot-square (5 m) cell. When he tried to stage a hunger strike, prison guards force-fed him.

Wang was released in 1993. He continued to write pro-democracy and human rights articles and was arrested again in 1995. He was charged with trying to overthrow the Chinese government and sentenced to eleven years in prison. But three years into the sentence, Wang was given a medical parole because of serious stomach problems. Chinese officials exiled Wang to the United States and forbade him from setting foot in mainland China.

In 2001 Wang received his master's degree from Harvard University in Massachusetts. In 2008 he received his doctorate. While studying at Harvard, Wang hung a poster of the Tank Man on his bedroom wall to "remind myself why I am here and what still needs to be done." Over the years, Wang has tried to return to China to visit his family, but each time he is refused entry.

The first student leader to be arrested from the most wanted list was Zhou Fengsuo, a student at Beijing's Tsinghua University. He was turned in to police by his sister and brother-in-law on June 13—the very day the list was issued. In pursuit of the other student leaders, the government posted public security officers in all airports and train stations and at border crossings. It instructed all local security bureaus to be on the lookout for the fugitive students. Within days, almost one-third of the wanted list was in custody. National TV showed images of the students being led into police stations and interrogated.

■ ■ ■ TRIED AND CONVICTED

By June 16, more than one thousand people around the country had been arrested. That day three workers who set fire to a train in Shanghai were tried and sentenced. No one died in the train fire, but the workers received the death penalty. In China, executions are carried out within days of sentencing. The convicted are shot in the head. The fact that the three men were workers might have played a part in the death penalty sentence. The government was very worried about workers going on strike, and the executions would send a clear message.

On June 17, eight Beijing residents were sentenced to death for attacking soldiers and burning vehicles during the crackdown. On June 20, the government revoked all exit visas—documents that allowed Chinese people to leave the country legally. The government was determined not to let any of the fugitives slip past.

On campus, students watched the arrests with alarm. They were not sure how far the government would go. It might arrest only the student leaders, or it might try to arrest anyone known to have taken part in demonstrations.

And yet, a streak of defiance remained on campus. In class, students were shown government propaganda praising the soldiers and condemning the violence of the counterrevolutionary riots. But students rejected such official stories and media accounts. As one student said, "We all know what really happened." Students were also required to attend political thought work sessions. In these sessions, they had to reflect on their role in the demonstrations and on how they could improve their thinking. In response, students adopted a "silence is golden" strategy. "'I don't know' became the answer to every question." And at night, under the cover of darkness, students wrote slogans on campus walls and hung posters.

After a long, tiring summer and fall, tensions began to fade. The government continued to arrest, try, and convict students and workers. With the student leaders gone, those left behind had no real plans for continuing the movement. Many students and Beijing residents began avoiding politics. They turned instead to studying, socializing, and working. The democracy movement had stalled.

CHAPTER 8

CHINA AFTER 1989

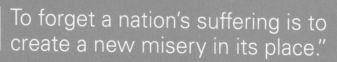

To forget a nation's suffering is to create a new misery in its place."

—Wang Dan, June 4 student protester, writing in 1998

Since 1961 a concrete wall had divided the European cities of East Berlin and West Berlin. But the Berlin Wall was more than a physical barrier. The wall separated Communist East Germany from democratic and free-market West Germany. The Berlin Wall was part of the Iron Curtain—the symbolic division between Soviet Communism and Western democracy.

Armed guards and barbed wire kept East German citizens from crossing the wall. But on November 9, 1989, the East German government announced that the wall was open. Amazed, East and West Berliners celebrated at the wall. People on both sides spent the next few weeks chipping away at the wall with axes and hammers. Dismantling the Berlin Wall was the first step in a series of events that many came to call the fall of Communism.

THE FALL OF COMMUNISM

Over the next two years, one-party Communist governments in Europe were replaced by elected, reform-minded leaders. The same

Germans tear down the Berlin Wall on November 10, 1989.

day the Berlin Wall opened, the Communist leader of Bulgaria, Todor Zhivkov, fell from power. On November 17, 1989, after several days of peaceful but widespread protests, the Communist government in Czechoslovakia resigned. After this so-called Velvet Revolution, civil rights advocate and reformer Vaclav Havel was elected president of Czechoslovakia. In December Romanian Communist dictator Nicolae Ceausescu was arrested and executed. In 1990 workers' rights champion Lech Walesa was elected president of Poland. Also in 1990, East and West Germany were reunified. And in 1991, the Soviet Union was dissolved and replaced with the Commonwealth of Independent States.

Chinese leaders watched the fall of Communism in Europe with unease. The CCP had managed to put down the June 4 pro-democracy movement. But there was still clearly a strong undercurrent of unrest in the country.

Deng Xiaoping had retired from all public offices immediately after the Tiananmen Square conflict. And the reformist faction led by Zhao Ziyang was gone from government. Li Peng and other party hard-liners took the opportunity to try to roll back some of Deng's economic plans. They believed that economic reforms had set the stage for the 1989

The election of leaders such as Lech Walesa *(above)* in Poland in the late 1980s signaled the end of Communism in Europe.

pro-democracy demonstrations. Such demonstrations and defiance, they said, would not have happened in the old Communist China. The hard-liners worked to slow the pace of economic reforms. They also returned to Marxist ideals and turned away from the idea of China's participation in the global market.

After Deng had lost direct influence in the new government, enough Deng and reform supporters still remained in government to split the Politburo. Deng found a new protégé in Zhu Rongji, a party official from Shanghai. Deng and Zhu began to look for allies among party officials in Shanghai and smaller cities. They argued that the hard-liners had been successful in slowing inflation, but continuing with the hard-liners' plan would damage new business. Deeper reforms, Deng argued, were needed to keep the Chinese economy from stagnating. Deng convinced the CCP that economic growth would actually prevent the fall of Communism in China. If the country were strong, secure, and wealthy, it would prove that the Communist Party offered the best leadership. And if individual citizens were successful and happy, they would be less likely to find fault with the government.

Deng also saw that the rift within the Chinese government would have to be healed. He argued that the CCP would not survive without economic reform. And economic reform could not be widely implemented without the CCP. Deng gathered together a group composed of political hard-liners, economic reformers, old-line party members, and military leaders. He convinced them to compromise and to support one another to get what they wanted.

Deng's proposed compromises were accepted, and the CCP announced in 1992 that it would officially establish a market economy. The old system of state-run factories and businesses would be shut down. But state-run operations could not be closed down until the millions of state workers had someplace else to go. To provide those new jobs, Deng focused on medium- and large-sized private companies. He would encourage enough new privately owned businesses to employ displaced state workers. Deng forged ahead with his plans. He was eighty-eight years old in 1992, but he set out on a long tour of China to ensure that reforms were in place in major Chinese cities.

■ WEALTH AND OPPORTUNITY

China's focus on economic growth has paid off. It has become the third-largest economy in the world, after the United States and Japan. Its economy is growing faster than any other. Since the early 1990s, China's gross domestic product (a basic measure of the size of a country's economy) has grown more than 10 percent each year. That growth has greatly reduced the country's poverty levels. In 1981, 53 percent of China's citizens were living below poverty levels. By 2001 that number had dropped to 8 percent.

The expanding economy has also given Chinese people a sense of self-determination—of being in control of their own lives. "In China, if you work hard, you have opportunities," says Wang Lichao. Wang is a younger cousin of 1989 student leader Wang Dan. He owns a telecommunications business in Beijing and lives in one of the city's new luxury high-rises. "When Wang Dan was a student, you had to depend on the state for a job, even if you were very talented. But now you can start your own business and look out for yourself."

The country's wealthy younger generation has changed urban China. Foreign luxury cars crowd the streets, and shopping malls are filled with expensive stores. Office workers in fashionable clothes chat on cell phones while they sip their iced mochas. They stock their homes with flat-screen TVs, the latest appliances and gadgets, and imported foods.

But not everyone has benefited equally. Workers hired by privately owned businesses benefit from a market economy. Successful companies compete for the best workers, and that drives wages up. But workers still employed at less efficient state-owned companies have not seen increasing wages. In fact, their standard of living is dropping. There is a growing sense that the best education, housing, and health care—all increasingly privatized rather than government-run—are out of their reach. And they worry that their children are falling farther and farther behind. This growing gap between the rich and the poor—especially in the face of Communism's promise of equality—exerts new pressure on the Chinese government.

Modern China struggles to bridge the gap between the wealthy and the poor.

◾ HUMAN AND CIVIL RIGHTS

Economic issues are not China's only problem. It continues to struggle with criticism over human and civil rights violations. As China became a bigger player in the global economy, it became answerable to the world community on these issues.

In 1951 Chinese forces occupied Tibet, an Asian territory north of the Himalayas. China regards Tibet as part of the PRC, but the Tibetan people have resisted Chinese rule. After occupation, Tibetans fought with Chinese forces. Tens of thousands died before the Chinese quelled the rebellion in 1959. Since then Tibetans have continued to look upon China as an illegal occupier. In March 2008, as China prepared to host the Summer Olympics, Tibetan monks staged a large anti-Chinese demonstration in Lhasa, Tibet's capital. Violence erupted between the demonstrators and the Chinese police. After sixteen people were killed in Lhasa, rioting spread to other parts of Tibet. Western countries hoped to use the Olympics as leverage in urging China to allow Tibetans more religious and cultural freedom. But the PRC refuses to change its policy.

Tibetan Buddhist monks stage an anti-Chinese demonstration in 2008.

China has also drawn criticism for its treatment of the Falun Gong movement. Falun Gong began in 1992 as a holistic (incorporating mind, body, and spirit) health system. It quickly became very popular and gained millions of followers. In 1999 Chinese authorities in the city of Tianjin arrested and beat Falun Gong members. In response, about fifteen thousand Falun Gong practitioners staged a peaceful protest on Beijing's Tiananmen Square. Following that protest, the Chinese government banned Falun Gong, calling it a dangerous cult that threatened China's internal stability. Thousands of Falun Gong members were arrested and sent to labor camps. Human rights organizations reported incidents of torture and death. Falun Gong supporters outside China continue to protest the treatment of practitioners.

Police stop a suspected Falun Gong member in Beijing in 1999.

In the area of civil rights, China has come under fire for censorship and a continued lack of democratic reforms. The number of foreign newspapers and television broadcasts available in China has grown. But the government still exercises far-reaching control of content. Undesirable news stories, such as the death of the moderate leader Zhao Ziyang in 2005, are blacked out. Controversial topics, such as Falun Gong or the 1989 student movement, are ignored altogether. And Internet censorship is extensive. China has an enormous number of Internet users, and the Chinese government recognizes the Internet's importance in business communications. But the government spends enormous resources monitoring Internet usage and blocking e-mail, search engines, and websites. Chinese Internet users who attempt to circulate or download forbidden information face prison or even death sentences.

As for democratic or political reforms, China does not seem much farther ahead than it was in 1989. Economic reforms may have diminished the government's control over people's employment and daily lives, but the CCP remains the country's sole political power. In December 2008, more than three hundred Chinese intellectuals called on the government to abandon Communism and institute a Western-style democracy. The CCP responded that "China would never adopt a multiparty political system." CCP leaders said the one-party system "was superior to the democratic model."

THE LEGACY OF TIANANMEN

Deng may have been correct about the power of economic growth to curb large-scale protests. The more secure and content people are in their own lives, the less likely they are to challenge the government. There have been no repeats of the 1989 demonstrations—nothing even close. In 2009 tens of thousands of Hong Kong residents marked the twentieth anniversary of Tiananmen Square with a candlelight vigil. But in Beijing, the day came and went with little public incident. Average Chinese people, said Chinese university professor Yuan Weishi, "don't want to destroy the social stability they are enjoying now."

After June 1989, Zhao Ziyang was placed under house arrest. He was never charged with a crime and was allowed to remain a CCP member. But for sixteen years, his home was watched by security forces. Visitors were carefully monitored. And when Zhao did go out, he was followed by police. Despite this surveillance, Zhao began making a series of secret audiotapes in 1999. The audiotapes recounted Zhao's memories of the 1989 demonstrations and his opinions on the government's actions. He passed the tapes to trusted friends, who smuggled them out of the house. The tapes—eventually numbering more than thirty—were collected by Bao Pu, the son of Zhao's one-time top aide, Bao Tong. The elder Bao spent six years in prison for his support of the 1989 student movement.

Zhao died in 2005, and Bao Pu worked on transcribing the tapes and gaining permission to publish from Zhao's heirs. In 2009 the memoirs were published as a book, *Prisoner of the State: The Secret Journal of Premier Zhao Ziyang*. The book details Zhao's opinion that the student demonstrations could have been easily solved by peaceful means and that the government's declaration of martial law was illegal. The book also argues that China's economic reforms were largely constructed by Zhao and his allies, rather than by Deng.

But if the average Chinese person is not haunted by the Tiananmen Square demonstrations, the Chinese government appears to be. The government continues to expend considerable energy in suppressing information or discussion about June 1989. Activists, writers, and foreign reporters who tried to commemorate the twentieth anniversary were

Writer and student leader Zhang Boli was among the last group to leave Tiananmen Square on June 4, 1989. He made his way back to his dorm room at Beijing University. From there, he and his wife, Li Yan, fled the city on bicycles, dodging tanks and gunfire.

In the city of Tianjin, the couple parted. Li returned home to their infant daughter, Xiao-xue. Zhang continued north. He did not want to leave China. He felt that he could wait out the government's reaction to the student protests. He believed that the June 4 demonstrations would bring about changes in China's leadership, and the student protesters would eventually be counted as heroes.

For almost two years, Zhang lived hidden in rural China. He moved often, not wanting to get those who helped him into trouble with police. He worked as a laborer and eventually built himself an isolated hut on a riverbank in northeastern China, near the border with Russia. He lived there with a pet dog, Little Tiger, and a young orphaned deer, Plum Blossom.

In winter 1991, Zhang realized that security forces were closing in on him. He risked returning to his hometown of Harbin to reunite

harassed or threatened by the government, according to the freedom-of-the-press organization Reporters Without Borders. Websites and Internet newsgroups about the Tiananmen Square uprising are blocked. Any news stories about the uprising must follow the government's version of events. Reporters and editors who violate that rule are fired.

with his family. But he learned that Li Yan wanted a divorce and had sent Xiao-xue to live with relatives. Zhang Boli managed one last secret meeting with his mother in Beijing before escaping to Hong Kong.

From Hong Kong, Zhang traveled to the United States and became a U.S. citizen. He remarried and had another child, Aaron. In the late 1990s, Zhang became a Christian minister. In 2001 the Chinese government allowed teenaged Xiao-xue to emigrate from China to the United States. Father and daughter were reunited after ten years. Zhang (*above in 2009*) and his family live in Fairfax, Virginia.

Schoolbooks and university lectures must also follow the government's version of events.

The government also still monitors the families of student leaders and those killed in June 1989. Relatives, medical personnel, and even soldiers who have asked the government for more information about

June 4 have been harassed by security forces and arrested. Students exiled after the events have had their requests to return to China repeatedly refused. Wang Dan, Chai Ling, Zhang Boli, and others have never returned to see family or friends. In October 2008, Zhou Yongjun, one of the students who knelt on the steps of the Great Hall on April 22, tried to sneak into China to visit his elderly, ill parents. He was arrested and remains in prison.

China has refused to reevaluate or discuss the government's response to the 1989 student movement—at least publicly. They maintain that China's success and prosperity are proof that the government handled the situation correctly. The effect of this lack of discussion has

The girlfriend of imprisoned Tiananmen activist Zhou Yongjun makes a plea for his release in 2009.

been that few young people in China understand the 1989 protests or know details about the military's actions. According to Human Rights Watch, an activist organization, at least three Western news organizations conducted an informal test on the matter in the 2000s. Reporters showed Beijing university students a photograph of Tank Man. Few recognized it. But for exiled student leaders, their families, Chinese intellectuals, and supporters around the world, the images from June 1989 remain a potent symbol of one of the major civil rights confrontations of modern times.

1912: During the Xinhai Revolution, rebels remove the last Chinese emperor, Pu Yi, from power. Rebel leader Sun Yat-sen founds the Kuomintang (KMT).

1919: The Treaty of Versailles, signed at the end of World War I, aggravates anti-Western sentiment in China. Thousands of Beijing students march in patriotic protest during the May Fourth Movement.

1921: The Chinese Communist Party (CCP) forms.

1927: The KMT and CCP begin waging violent battles against each other.

1946: Following the end of World War II, the struggle between the KMT and the CCP grows into a civil war.

1949: The CCP defeats the KMT. CCP leader Mao Zedong announces the founding of the People's Republic of China (PRC). The KMT flees to Taiwan.

1956: Mao begins his Hundred Flowers Campaign to encourage intellectual freedom. He ends the campaign within a year when intellectuals criticize his leadership.

1958: Mao begins the Great Leap Forward, an attempt to solve China's economic problems. The five-year-long plan ends in disaster for the Chinese people. In response, CCP members urge Mao to take a more moderate approach to Communism.

1966: Mao begins the Cultural Revolution to purge moderates from the CCP and reassert his power over the party. Thousands are killed or imprisoned during the ten-year campaign.

1976: Mao dies. Hua Guofeng becomes chairman of the CCP and welcomes moderates back into government.

1978: Deng Xiaoping forces Hua from office and takes over leadership of the CCP. Deng begins a campaign to repair China's economy and reform the CCP. He opens a Democracy Wall in Beijing to encourage the public to express opinions about the government.

1979: Deng closes the Democracy Wall and arrests its most famous activist, Wei Jingsheng.

1980: Deng protégé and economic reformer Zhao Ziyang becomes premier of the PRC.

1981: Deng protégé and economic reformer Hu Yaobang becomes general secretary of the CCP.

1986: Disappointed by the pace of social and political reforms, tens of thousands of Chinese students march in protest.

1987: Party officials criticize Hu Yaobang for not publicly condemning the 1986 student protests. Hu is forced to resign from office. Zhao Ziyang becomes the CCP general secretary, and hard-liner Li Peng is appointed PRC premier. The government launches Anti-Spiritual Pollution and Anti-Bourgeois Liberalization campaigns.

1989:

April 15 Hu Yaobang dies suddenly. Students begin gathering on Chinese campuses to pay tribute to him.

April 17   The memorial gatherings become increasingly emotional and political. In Beijing, students move off campuses to gather in Tiananmen Square.

April 18   Beijing University students lead an enormous march through the city to the square. At the square, they announce a list of seven demands for the government. Several hundred students begin a sit-in in front of the Great Hall of the People.

April 19   Students stage a sit-in at the Xinhua Gate entrance to Zhongnanhai. Beijing city officials begin sending police to Tiananmen Square and Xinhua Gate to keep order.

April 20   Fights break out between police and demonstrators at Xinhua Gate. Some students return to campuses and announce to crowds that police had beaten them. Students call the event the Xinhua Gate Bloody Incident. They begin organizing class boycotts and more protests. Student leaders form the Beida Solidarity Student Union Preparatory Committee and the Autonomous Federation of Students.

April 21   About fifty thousand Beijing students gather on Tiananmen Square for a rally. Thousands of students begin arriving in Beijing from other Chinese cities.

April 22   Hu Yaobang's funeral is held in the Great Hall of the People. After the funeral, student leaders kneel on the steps of the hall to present their list of demands to Li Peng. Li Peng refuses to appear. The incident garners the students sympathy among Beijing citizens.

April 23   Zhao Ziyang leaves for a state visit to North Korea. Li Peng takes over leadership of government discussions about the student movement.

April 24 Li Peng and other CCP hard-liners convince Deng Xiaoping that the student protests are turning into an antigovernment movement.

April 26 Party leadership publishes an editorial in the *People's Daily* labeling the student movement "turmoil." Students and citizens react angrily.

April 27 Fifty thousand students rally at Tiananmen Square. They are joined by students protesting in several other major cities.

April 28 Li Peng publishes another editorial claiming that a small group of black hands—antigovernment troublemakers—are leading students astray. The CCP urges school and university officials to step up pro-Communist thought work on campus.

April 29 Government official Yuan Mu holds a dialogue with students. Students blast the dialogue session as rigged.

April 30 Zhao Ziyang returns from North Korea to find that almost 70 percent of Beijing university students are boycotting classes. International media coverage of the student movement increases.

May 1 Zhao and Li Peng clash over how to handle the demonstrations. Zhao defends students but admits that public security has become an issue.

May 2 Students from forty schools meet at Beijing University to form a Beijing Student Dialogue Delegation. They finalize a second list of demands and send it to the Politburo Standing Committee.

May 3 Yuan Mu publicly rejects the list and declares the dialogue delegation illegal. Zhao makes a speech praising the students but asking them to go back to class. Students announce that as a compromise, they will demonstrate once more and then return to classes.

May 4 Students celebrate the anniversary of the 1919 student movement with a march on Tiananmen Square. Student leaders read a May Fourth Declaration asserting their commitment to democratic reforms. Zhao Ziyang meets with foreign investors from the Asian Development Bank and assures them that the student movement is not opposed to the CCP. Student demonstrations begin to wind down.

May 11 Some student leaders discuss their mistrust of the government's intention to continue reform work and the need to reenergize the student movement. They decide to stage a hunger strike.

May 12 Student leader Chai Ling's emotional speech at Beijing University recruits students for the hunger strike.

May 13 Government leadership learns of the student hunger strike. Yan Mingfu, an ally of Zhao Ziyang, meets with students. He asks them to show patriotism and not embarrass China during an upcoming visit from Russian leader Mikhail Gorbachev. Student leaders agree to leave Tiananmen Square before Gorbachev's visit. On the square, the hunger strike begins.

May 14 Supporters of the hunger strikers crowd Tiananmen Square. CCP hard-liners argue to Deng that Zhao Ziyang is creating an obvious rift in party leadership. Yan Mingfu holds another dialogue session with student leaders, but the meeting quickly breaks apart. The hunger strikers announce that they will not leave the square.

May 15   Gorbachev arrives. Foreign media in Beijing to cover his visit turn their attention to the hunger strikers.

May 16   Zhao meets with Gorbachev and explains Deng Xiaoping's continuing influence on the CCP.

May 17   In Beijing a crowd of two million people forms the largest demonstration in PRC history. Demonstrations also occur in twenty other Chinese cities. Protesters call for Deng to step down and Li Peng to resign. At a Politburo meeting, Li Peng convinces Deng that Zhao has allowed the student movement to grow into a serious public security threat. Deng agrees to declare martial law in Beijing. Zhao attempts to resign, but the resignation is rejected.

May 18   Zhao visits the hunger strikers in the square and begs them not to endanger their lives. He attends one last Politburo meeting before pleading illness.

May 19   The People's Liberation Army (PLA) begins moving troops in preparation for martial law. Beijing factory workers threaten to go on strike in support of the student movement. Students from other Chinese cities continue to pour into Beijing. Student leadership becomes divided as news reaches the square of impending martial law.

May 20   The government declares martial law in central Beijing. Troops begin moving into the city from the suburbs.

May 21   Students from outside Beijing throw their support behind a new leadership group, Defend Tiananmen Square Headquarters. The group votes to continue the hunger strike even in the face of martial law. On the streets, Beijing residents begin blocking troop movements into the city.

May 23 Martial law troops retreat to the suburbs. But rumors begin that soldiers are infiltrating the city in street clothes. In reaction to the martial law declaration, international leaders urge China to find a peaceful solution. On Tiananmen Square, three protesters deface the portrait of Chairman Mao.

May 27 Jiang Zemin is appointed CCP general secretary. Activists in Hong Kong hold the Concert for Democracy in China, raising millions of Hong Kong dollars for the Beijing student movement.

May 29 Beijing police arrest leaders of the Autonomous Federation of Workers. Students erect the Goddess of Democracy statue on the square.

May 31 Students begin a cleanup of the square. The CCP organizes pro-government rallies in Beijing. Thousands of students rally in support of the arrested workers.

June 2 Writer Liu Xiaobo and three others organize their own hunger strike. Their speeches draw large crowds to Tiananmen Square. The government orders martial law troops back into the city to clear protesters from Tiananmen Square.

June 3 PLA troops moving into Beijing clash with protesting residents. Hospitals begin filling with the wounded. Residents and soldiers are killed as the clashes grow increasingly violent.

June 4 PLA troops surround Tiananmen Square. Liu Xiaobo leads a delegation to negotiate a student withdrawal. As students file out, military vehicles flood the square. Outside Tiananmen, tanks fire on retreating students. The Chinese government announces that it has ended the counterrevolutionary riots in Beijing. Across China and in many other countries, protesters denounce the deaths in Beijing.

June 5 World leaders react to the forceful clearing of Tiananmen Square. In Beijing, student leaders and other activists prepare to flee China. Parents begin showing up at Tiananmen to look for missing children. On Chang'an Boulevard, foreign photographers snap pictures of a lone protester stepping out in front of a line of army tanks. Images of Tank Man appear in publications and on TV around the world.

June 6 Foreign embassies in China begin urging their citizens to leave.

June 7 The government announces its toll of dead and injured. Human rights groups denounce the tolls, claiming that the reports greatly underestimate civilian deaths.

June 8 Li Peng appears on national TV to thank the PLA.

June 9 Deng Xiaoping appears on national TV and calls for a moment of silence for the military's "deceased martyrs."

June 12 The government bans all autonomous student and labor organizations. It calls on all Chinese citizens to report any counterrevolutionary activities.

June 13 The government issues a most wanted list for twenty-one student leaders. The first student from the list, Zhou Fengsuo, is arrested.

June 16 The number of people arrested in connection with the demonstrations exceeds one thousand. Three workers in Shanghai are sentenced to death.

June 17	Eight Beijing residents are sentenced to death.
June 20	The government revokes all travel visas to prevent student leaders from escaping the country.
November 9	The opening of the Berlin Wall in Germany marks the beginning of the fall of Communism in Europe.

1992: Deng Xiaoping continues with his economic reform plans with a tour of China.

1999: At the tenth anniversary of the 6/4 student movement, Chinese officials maintain that the government handled the student demonstrations correctly.

2001: The poverty level in China drops to its lowest in modern history.

2008: China hosts the Summer Olympics in Beijing.

2009: The twentieth anniversary of the 6/4 student movement passes without incident.

Chai Ling

(b. 1966) In 1989 Chai Ling was a twenty-three-year-old
graduate student, studying child psychology at Beijing Normal
University. Near the end of the 1989 demonstrations, Chai led
the student hunger strike. She is often portrayed as an emotional
and controversial leader. After the Tiananmen Square crackdown,
Chai was named on the government's most wanted list of student
leaders. She and her husband, Feng Congde, went into hiding in
China. They escaped through Hong Kong to France. Chai then
moved to the United States to attend Princeton and Harvard
universities. She and Feng divorced, and Chai started a software
company, Jenzabar, with her second husband, Robert Maginn. In
2007 she launched the Jenzabar Foundation, pledging $1 million
to support democratic activities in China.

Deng Xiaoping

(1904–1997) Deng was the leader of the CCP from the end
of the Cultural Revolution in 1976 until his retirement in
1989. He was born in central China to a well-to-do family.
During and after World War II, he rose through the ranks of the
Communist Party. He was purged from power twice but came
back to replace Mao Zedong as CCP leader. Deng then oversaw
the transformation of China from a chaotic revolutionary state
to a world power. In healing China's wounds from the Cultural
Revolution, he greatly improved the country's military and
its educational system. Deng was also dedicated to economic
reforms. But he was loyal to the CCP and to the Communist
model of a one-party state. During the 1989 student movement,
Deng sided with party hard-liners and approved the decision
to declare martial law. He retired in the wake of the 1989
Tiananmen Square confrontation but continued his economic

reforms. He died in February 1997 from complications of
Parkinson's disease.

Feng Congde

(b. 1967) Feng was twenty-two and studying physics at Beijing
University in spring 1989. He and his wife, Chai Ling, became
student leaders on Tiananmen Square that spring. After being
named on the most wanted list, the couple hid in rural China
until they could escape to Hong Kong. They traveled to Paris,
France. The couple divorced, and Feng remained in Paris. He
continued his graduate studies and his activism on behalf of
democracy in China. He is among the Chinese exiles calling for
the release of June 4 students still in prison and for the pardon
of all students who remain on the most wanted list.

Hu Yaobang

(1915–1989) From 1980 until 1987, Hu was the Communist
Party general secretary. Following large-scale student
demonstrations in the fall of 1986, Hu was criticized by party
hard-liners for sympathizing with student activists. On January
16, he was forced to resign in disgrace and thereby became a
hero to Chinese students. He died following a heart attack on
April 15, 1989. His death and funeral are seen as the catalyst for
the Tiananmen Square demonstrations in the spring and summer
of 1989.

Li Peng

(b. 1928) As a boy, Li Peng was adopted by Zhou Enlai,
Communist China's first premier. As a young adult, Li studied
engineering in the Soviet Union for several years before
returning to China in 1954. Using his engineering background,

he worked in China's electric and water power industries. He also moved up the ranks of the Communist Party and in 1983 was appointed to the Politburo. In 1987 he was named China's premier. A hard-line defender of Communist policy, Li refused to take a moderate approach to the 1989 student demonstrations. He became a focal point of the students' anger and frustration with the government. After the army crushed the student movement, Li served a second term as premier until 1998. He remained influential within the party but was deeply unpopular with the public. He retired from politics in 2002.

Mao Zedong

(1893–1976) Mao Zedong was a young revolutionary at the founding of the CCP in 1921. By the 1949 founding of the PRC, Mao was the party's powerful leader. He was dedicated to the ideals and strategies of the Marxist revolution. He often let his protégés handle the practical matters of government while he developed a charismatic leadership. In pursuing revolutionary ideals, he pushed China into a series of economic, political, and social disasters that culminated with the Cultural Revolution. His policies cost millions of lives and brought China to the brink of collapse. Yet he is remembered in China as the person who led the country to independence from foreign interference. He died in September 1976 after a series of heart attacks. His body was laid to rest in a mausoleum on Tiananmen Square.

Wang Dan

(b. 1969) Twenty-year-old Beijing University history student Wang Dan was one of the main student leaders in the 1989 demonstrations. Immediately after the June 4 crackdown, he went into hiding, waiting for a chance to escape China. But he decided to return to Beijing. He was arrested and spent four years in prison. He was released, rearrested, and returned to prison before being sent into exile in the United States. He earned a doctorate at Harvard University and continues to lecture and write in support of democracy in China. In 2009 Wang traveled to Taiwan to teach history at Chengchi University as a visiting scholar. He has tried to enter mainland China to visit his family, but the Chinese government refuses to let him in.

Wuer Kaixi

(b. 1968) Wuer was in his first year at Beijing Normal University when he joined the 1989 student movement. He quickly became a student leader. Wuer was part of the core of students who decided strategy, rallied demonstrators, attended government dialogues, and met with the media. Attractive and charismatic, he drew the attention of reporters and photographers. He strongly disagreed with the student decision to go on a hunger strike, and on May 22, he was expelled from the square. After soldiers crushed the student demonstration on June 4, Wuer was named on the government's most-wanted list. He escaped from China through Hong Kong and fled to France and then the United States. In the late 1990s, he moved to Taiwan, where he works as a political commentator. He has expressed hopes to return to his homeland, but he cannot without risking arrest. He remains the second most-wanted criminal in China for his role in the 1989 demonstrations.

Zhang Boli

(b. 1959) At twenty-nine, Zhang Boli was one of the oldest student leaders in 1989. He had worked a few years as a journalist and returned to Beijing University as a graduate student. As a leader on Tiananmen Square, Zhang was moderate and thoughtful. He remained on the square to the last, witnessing the PLA soldiers driving students out with guns and tanks. Named on the government's most wanted list, Zhang fled north to the Chinese countryside. He intended to cross into the Soviet Union but ended up living outside an isolated Chinese village for almost two years. In 1991 he escaped through Hong Kong to the United States. He married and became a Christian minister. He and his family settled in Virginia.

Zhao Ziyang

(1919–2005) Zhao was born into a wealthy family in central China and joined the Communist Party as a teenager. He was denounced during the Cultural Revolution. His return to politics was supported by Zhou Enlai and Deng Xiaoping. With Deng as his mentor, Zhao joined the Politburo in the late 1970s. At the peak of his career, he was China's premier (1980–1987) and general secretary of the Communist Party (1987–1989). In favor of modernization and reform, Zhao was the government's moderate voice during the 1989 student demonstrations. He urged Communist leadership to hold dialogues with student leaders. But his sympathy for the students was seized upon as disloyalty to the party. As party hard-liners began to organize a military response to the student demonstrations, Zhao withdrew from his duties. After June 1989, he remained under house arrest in Beijing for sixteen years. In 2009, four years after his death, his memoirs were published by his friend Bao Pu. The memoirs revealed that Zhao had never changed his opinion that the Chinese government made a serious error in how it handled the 1989 student movement.

autocracy: government by a single ruler with unlimited power

autonomous: in modern Chinese politics, refers to organizations not approved or overseen by the Communist Party

black hand: referring to secret forces, especially foreign ones, allegedly working to undermine the Communist government

bourgeois: having to do with the middle class (bourgeoisie) and values such as personal wealth, social status, and property ownership

boycott: a protest involving a refusal to participate, such as a refusal to attend classes or buy certain items

bureaucracy: an extensive network of government officials

capitalism: an economic system based on private (as opposed to government) ownership, competition in the marketplace, and prices based on supply and demand

Chinese Communist Party: the dominant political party in modern China, founded in 1921

civil rights: fundamental freedoms that guarantee the exercise of the privileges of citizenship and equal protection under the law. Free speech, freedom of religion, freedom of the press, and the right to vote are examples of civil rights.

Communism: a political theory in which social and economic classes are abolished and all people are regarded as equals. Communism also refers to a political party or system of government operating on the principles of Communism.

counterrevolution: a rebellion against revolutionary forces

Cultural Revolution: from 1966 to 1976, a campaign to rid Chinese society of anything that belonged to the pre-Communist way of life

dazibao: handwritten Chinese wall posters lettered with large characters, used to publicly announce something or express a political opinion

democracy: a system of government in which citizens have a direct say through free elections and political representation

dongluan: Chinese for "turmoil" or "chaos," often used to describe political violence and mayhem

duihua: the Chinese word for "dialogue"

elders: in Communist China, an informal group of longtime party members who act as advisers

Four Modernizations: in modern Chinese political thought, changes in agriculture, industry, defense, and technology that would make China a global power

free market: of an economic system, based on the laws of supply and demand, with little government interference

Gang of Four: Jiang Qing (Mao's wife), Zhang Chunqiao, Yao Wenyuan, and Wang Hongwen—enforcers of Mao's policies during the Cultural Revolution

Great Leap Forward: from 1958 to 1962, Mao's attempt to solve China's economic problems by increasing government control of agriculture and rapidly developing industrialization

Hundred Flowers Campaign: from 1956 to 1957, an effort by Mao Zedong to encourage intellectual freedom

imperialism: rule by an emperor, or the extension of political and economic control of one country over another

intellectual: in Chinese society, someone who makes a living writing, teaching, studying, or researching

Kuomintang (KMT): a Chinese political party founded in 1912. The KMT is also known as the Nationalist Party.

Leninism: a variation of Marxism developed by Vladimir Lenin in the early 1900s. Lenin argued that a workers' rebellion against capitalism must be led by a professional political party of Socialist revolutionaries.

martial law: an emergency measure adopted by a government during a crisis, in which the military takes control of police and security duties in a specific area

Marxism: political theory based on the nineteenth-century writings of Karl Marx and Friedrich Engels. Marx believed that as the exploitation of workers under capitalism increased, workers would revolt and establish a Socialist society

May Fourth Movement: a student uprising held on May 4, 1919, in protest of the Treaty of Versailles, which had brought an end to World War I

National People's Congress (NPC): the legislative, or lawmaking, branch of the People's Republic of China

People's Liberation Army (PLA): the military force organized from the Red Army after the founding of the People's Republic of China

People's Republic of China (PRC): the Chinese government founded by the Chinese Communist Party after it defeated the Kuomintang in 1949

Politburo: the policymaking committee of the Chinese Communist Party

propaganda: information distributed by an organization or a government to persuade an audience to think or behave a certain way

purge: to strip of political power or expel from an organization

Red Army: the military force organized by the Chinese Communist Party during World War II

Red Guards: in the 1960s and 1970s, young Chinese supporters of Mao's Cultural Revolution

republic: a form of government with elected leaders

revolution: a sudden and radical overthrow of a government or an established system

Socialism: an economic and political theory in which the government controls the production and distribution of goods. According to some Communist theory, Socialism is a transitional step between capitalism and Communism.

spiritual pollution: in Chinese Communism, the influence of Western capitalist ideas

thought work: formal meetings or private conversations led by Communist Party members to ensure that others are correctly following Communist ideology

World War I: from 1914 to 1918, a major international conflict between the Central powers (Germany, the Austro-Hungarian Empire, and other powers) and the Allies (France, Great Britain, Japan, Russia, the United States, and other nations)

World War II: from 1939 to 1945, a major international conflict between the Axis (Germany, Japan, and other nations) and the Allies (China, France, Great Britain, Russia, the United States, and other nations)

Xinhai Revolution: a 1912 rebellion in China that forced the last emperor, Pu Yi, from power

SOURCE NOTES

8 Mao Zedong, "On the Correct Handling of Contradictions among People," quoted in *Quotations from Chairman Mao Tsetung* (San Francisco: China Books, 1990), 142.

24 Janice Castro, ed., "The Last Emperor," Time.com, http://www.time.com/time/deng/leader09.html, 1997 (January 30, 2010).

26 Wei Jingsheng, "The Fifth Modernization," available online at http://www.echonyc.com/~wei/Fifth.html (January 22, 2010).

26 Ibid.

32 Fang Lizhi, quoted in Orville Schell, "China's Andrei Sakharov," *Atlantic Online*, May 1988, http://www.theatlantic.com/unbound/flashbks/china/fang.htm (April 4, 2009).

37–38 Zhang Boli, *Escape from China* (New York: Washington Square Press, 1998), 28–29.

40 Shen Tong, *Almost a Revolution*, with Marianne Yen (Boston: Houghton Mifflin, 1990), 120.

41 Fang Lizhi, quoted in Schell, "China's Andrei Sakharov."

43 "Democracy Wall," in *The Gate of Heavenly Peace*, available online at http://www.tsquare.tv/wall (January 22, 2010).

46 Zhang Liang, *The Tiananmen Papers*, eds. Andrew J. Nathan and Perry Link (New York: PublicAffairs, 2001), 30.

47 Shen, *Almost a Revolution*, 167.

47 "Hu Yaobang—April 1989," in *The Gate of Heavenly Peace*, transcript, http://www.tsquare.tv/film/transhu.html (January 22, 2010).

48 Zhang Liang, *The Tiananmen Papers*, 27.

54 Ibid., 30.

55 "Hu Yaobang—April 1989."

55 Dingxin Zhao, *The Power of Tiananmen: State-Society Relations and the 1989 Beijing Student Movement* (Chicago: University of Chicago Press, 2001), 150.

55 Zhang Liang, *The Tiananmen Papers*, 29.

55 Ibid., 31.

58 Ibid., 22.

58 Zhang Boli, *Escape from China*, 37.

59 Zhang Liang, *The Tiananmen Papers*, 30.

59 "Hu Yaobang—April 1989."

60 *People's Daily*, editorial, April 26, 1989, quoted in *Ming Pao News, June Four: A Chronicle of the Chinese Democratic Uprising*, trans. Zi Jin and Qin Zhou (Fayetteville: University of Arkansas Press, 1989), 27.

61 Zhang Liang, *The Tiananmen Papers*, 53.

61 Ibid., 57.

61 Zhang Liang, *The Tiananmen Papers*, 62.

63 *People's Daily*, "It Is Necessary to Take a Clear-Cut Stand against Disturbances," editorial, April 26, 1989, available online at http://www.tsquare.tv/chronology/April26ed.html (January 22, 2010).

63 "It Is Necessary To Take A Clear-Cut Stand Against Disturbances," editorial in the *People's Daily*, April 26, 1989. Reprinted at http://www.tsquare.tv/chronology/April26ed.html.

64 Zhang Liang, *The Tiananmen Papers*, 76.

65 Ibid.

66 *Ming Pao News, June Four: A Chronicle of the Chinese Democratic Uprising*, trans. Zi Jin and Qin Zhou (Fayetteville: University of Arkansas Press, 1989), 37.

67 Zhang Liang, *The Tiananmen Papers*, 96.

71 Ibid.

72 "May 4," in *The Gate of Heavenly Peace*, transcript, http://www.tsquare.tv/film/transmay4.html (January 22, 2010).

73 Dingxin, *The Power of Tiananmen*, 288.

73 Zhang Liang, *The Tiananmen Papers*, 154

76 Shen, *Almost a Revolution*, 247.

76 "Hunger Strike," in *The Gate of Heavenly Peace*, transcript, http://www.tsquare.tv/film/transhs.html (January 22, 2010).

80 Zhang Liang, *The Tiananmen Papers*, 177.

82 Ibid., 189.

84 Nicholas D. Kristof, "Chinese Students, in About-Face, Will Continue Occupying Square," *New York Times*, May 30, 1989, http://www.nytimes.com/1989/05/30/world/chinese-students-in-about-face-will-continue-occupying-square.html?scp=21&sq=Kristof+Tiananmen+Square&st=nyt (January 22, 2010).

85 Andrew Walder, quoted in Dingxin Zhao, *The Power of Tiananmen*, 173.

89 "Martial Law," in *The Gate of Heavenly Peace*, transcript, http://www.tsquare.tv/film/transml.html (January 30, 2010).

89 Shen, *Almost a Revolution*, 301.

96 Liu Xiaobo, Zhou Tuo, Hou Deijian, and Gao Xin, "Hunger Strike Declaration" quoted in *Ming Pao News*, 137.

97 Zhang Liang, *The Tiananmen Papers*, 358

98 "June 4," in *The Gate of Heavenly Peace*, transcript, available online at http://www.tsquare.tv/film/transjune4.html (January 30, 2010).

100 National Security Archive, Tiananmen Square, 1989: *The Declassified History*, n.d., http://www.gwu.edu/~nsarchiv/NSAEBB/NSAEBB16/documents/10-02.htm (January 22, 2010).

102 Jan Wong, *Red China Blues* (New York: Anchor Books, 1996), 249.

103 BBC, "Witnessing Tiananmen: Clearing the Square," *BBC News*, June 4, 2004, http://news.bbc.co.uk/2/hi/asia-pacific/3775907.stm (March 22, 2009).

103 "June 4," in *The Gate of Heavenly Peace*, transcript.

104 Zhang Boli, *Escape from China*, 1.

104–105 BBC, "Witnessing Tiananmen."

105 HRIC, "Testimony of Fang Zheng, wounded," *Human Rights in China*, January 31, 1999, http://www.hrichina.org/public/contents/article?revision%5fid=1798&item%5fid=1797 (January 22, 2010).

105 Zhang Liang, *The Tiananmen Papers*, 387.

106 George H. W. Bush, quoted in Robert L. Suettinger, *Beyond Tiananmen: The Politics of U.S.-China Relations, 1989–2000* (Washington, DC: Brookings Institute, 2003), 66.

107 BBC, "1989: Massacre in Tiananmen Square," *BBC News*, June 4, 1989, http://news.bbc.co.uk/onthisday/hi/dates/stories/june/4/newsid_2496000/2496277.stm (March 22, 2009).

107 Robert D. McFadden, "The West

Condemns the Crackdown," *New York Times*, June 5, 1989, http://www.nytimes.com/1989/06/05/world/the-west-condemns-the-crackdown.html?scp=1&sq=&st=nyt (August 30, 2009).

108 Wong, *Red China Blues*, 263.

110 Gary Pranger, telephone interview with author, May 17, 2009.

111 Ibid.

113 Zhang Liang, *The Tiananmen Papers*, 425.

114 Nicholas D. Kristof, "Turmoil in China; China Tightens Grip with a Ban on Groups Calling for Democracy," *New York Times*, June 13, 1989, http://www.nytimes.com/1989/06/13/world/turmoil-in-china-china-tightens-grip-with-a-ban-on-groups-calling-for-democracy.html?scp=6&sq=&st=nyt (August 30, 2009).

114 Ibid.

114 Zhang Boli, *Escape from China*, 52.

114 Wang Dan, "A Cry for Democracy Ends in Bloodshed," TimeAsia.com, September 27, 1999, http://www.time.com/time/asia/magazine/99/0927/tiananmen.html (January 22, 2010).

114 Wang Dan, *Prison Memoirs*, quoted in Li Shuxian, acceptance speech for 1998 Democracy Award, National Endowment for Democracy, May 2, 2008, http://www.ned.org/events/demaward/demaward1998-danspeech.html (January 22, 2010).

115 "Tiananmen Twenty Years On," Index on Censorship, April 15, 2009, http://www.indexoncensorship.org/2009/04/15/tiananmen-twenty-years-on/ (January 22, 2010).

115 Hannah Beech, "The Exile and the Entrepreneur," TimeAsia.com, May 31, 2004, http://www.time.com/time/asia/covers/501040607/story4.html (January 22, 2010).

116 Associated Press, "Chinese Student Gets 9 Years for Role in Protest," *New York Times*, August 29, 1989, http://www.nytimes.com/1989/08/29/world/chinese-student-gets-9-years-for-role-in-protest.html?scp=1&sq=&st=nyt (January 22, 2010).

117 Zhang Liang, *The Tiananmen Papers*, 454.

118 Wang Dan, foreword to Zhang Boli, *Escape from China* (New York: Washington Square Press, 1998; English language translation, 2002).

122 Beech, "The Exile and the Entrepreneur."

126 Michael Wines, "In China, No Plans to Emulate the West's Way," *New York Times*, March 9, 2009, intl. sect.

126 Ibid.

126 Michael Wines, "China Is on Edge over Anniversaries of Volatile Points in Its History," *New York Times*, March 9, 2009, intl. sect.

130 HRIC, "Testimony of Zhou Shuzhuang, mother of Duan Changlong," Human Rights in China, January 31, 1999, http://www.hrichina.org/public/contents/article?revision%5fid=3610&item%5fid=3609 (January 22, 2010).

AsiaNews. "Twenty Years Since Tiananmen Massacre: China Restricts Entry Visas." *AsiaNews.it*, March, 11, 2009. http://www.asianews.it/index .php?l=en&art=14692&size=A (March 22, 2009).

BBC. "1989: Massacre in Tiananmen Square." BBC News, June 4, 1989. http://news .bbc.co.uk/onthisday/hi/dates/stories/june/4/newsid_2496000/2496277.stm (March 22, 2009).

———. "Picture Power: Tiananmen Stand-Off." BBC News, October 7, 2005. http:// news.bbc.co.uk/2/hi/asia-pacific/4313282.stm (March 22, 2009).

———. "Where Are They Now?" BBC News, June 2, 1999. http://news.bbc. co.uk/2/hi/special_report/1999/06/99/tiananmen_square/359133.stm (August 30, 2009).

———. "Witnessing Tiananmen: Clearing the Square." BBC News, June 4, 2004. http://news.bbc.co.uk/2/hi/asia-pacific/3775907.stm (March 22, 2009).

Black, Jane. "High-Tech Tiananmen Still a Long Way Off." BBC News, June 2, 1999. http://news.bbc.co.uk/2/hi/special_report/1999/06/99/tiananmen_ square/354499.stm (March 22, 2009).

Bodeen, Christopher. "Rights Group: Ex-Soldier Who Voiced Regrets Over Role in 1989 Tiananmen Crackdown Detained." ABC News, March 20, 2009. http:// abcnews.go.com/International/wireStory?id=7129205 (August 30, 2009).

China's Cultural Revolution: A Brief Overview. Adapted from William A. Joseph, "Cultural Revolution." In *The Oxford Companion to Politics of the World.* 2nd ed. Edited by Joel Krieger, William A. Joseph, et al. New York: Oxford University Press, 2001. Available online at http://www.wellesley.edu/Polisci/wj/China1972/brief -intro.htm (March 22, 2009).

CNN. "China's Dissidents: Division in the Ranks." CNN.com, June 3, 1999. http:// www.cnn.com/WORLD/asiapcf/9906/02/tiananmen/tiananmen.dissidents/ index.html (March 22, 2009).

———. "Visions of China." CNN.com. 2001. http://www.cnn.com/ SPECIALS/1999/china.50 (April 4, 2009).

Gifford, Rob. "How the West Was Lost." BBC News, June 2, 1999. http://news .bbc.co.uk/2/hi/special_report/1999/06/99/tiananmen_square/359000.stm (March 22, 2009).

———. "Student Division Leads Tiananmen Failure." BBC News, June 3, 1999. http://news.bbc.co.uk/2/hi/special_report/1999/06/99/tiananmen _square/360042.stm (March 22, 2009).

Kristof, Nicholas D. "Turmoil in China; China Tightens Grip with a Ban on Groups Calling for Democracy." *New York Times*, June 13, 1989. http://www.nytimes .com/1989/06/13/world/turmoil-in-china-china-tightens-grip-with-a-ban-on-groups-calling-for-democracy.html (August 30, 2009).

Long Bow Group. *The Gate of Heavenly Peace*. Transcript. 1995. Available online at http://www.tsquare.tv/film/transcript01.html (March 22, 2009).

Marti, Michael E. *China and the Legacy of Deng Xiaoping*. Washington, DC: Brassey's, 2002.

McFadden, Robert D. "The West Condemns the Crackdown." *New York Times*, June 5, 1989. http://www.nytimes.com/1989/06/05/world/the-west-condemns-the-crackdown.html?sec=&spon= (August 30, 2009).

Miles, James. "Dissidence Then and Now." BBC News, June 2, 1999. http://news.bbc.co.uk/2/hi/programmes/from_our_own_correspondent/358303.stm (March 22, 2009).

———. "Tiananmen: The Birth of Economic Revolution." BBC News, June 4, 2000. http://news.bbc.co.uk/2/hi/special_report/1999/06/99/tiananmen_square/358399.stm (March 22, 2009).

Schell, Orville. "Analyzing the Tiananmen Papers." Time.com, January 15, 2001. http://www.time.com/time/asia/magazine/2001/0115/tiananmen.view.html (March 22, 2009).

———. "China's Agony of Defeat." *Newsweek*, August 4, 2008, 39–41.

———. "China's Andrei Sakharov." *Atlantic*, May 1988. http://www.theatlantic.com/unbound/flashbks/china/fang.htm (April 4, 2009).

Time. "How Many Really Died?" Time.com, June 4, 1990. http://www.time.com/time/magazine/article/0,9171,970278,00.html (March 22, 2009).

Wei Jingsheng. *The Courage to Stand Alone*. New York: Viking, 1997.

Zhang Liang. *The Tiananmen Papers*. Edited by Andrew J. Nathan and Perry Link. Afterword by Orville Schell. New York: PublicAffairs, 2001.

Zhao, Dingxin. *The Power of Tiananmen: State-Society Relations and the 1989 Beijing Student Movement*. Chicago: University of Chicago Press, 2001.

Zi Jin and Qin Zhou, trans. *Ming Pao News. June Four: A Chronicle of the Chinese Democratic Uprising*. Fayetteville: University of Arkansas Press, 1989.

Behnke, Alison. *China in Pictures*. Minneapolis: Twenty-First Century Books, 2003. This book provides an introduction to the history, culture, and people of China.

Boli, Zhang. *Escape from China*. New York: Washington Square Press, 1998. Student leader Zhang Boli details his life on the run following the 1989 demonstrations on Tiananmen Square.

Fenby, Jonathan. *Modern China: The Fall and Rise of a Great Power, 1850 to the Present*. New York: Ecco, 2008. Journalist Jonathan Fenby looks at the historical forces that have shaped contemporary China. Divided into six parts, the book begins with the decline of imperial China and ends with the modern leadership of Jiang Zemin and Hu Jintao.

"The Gate of Heavenly Peace." http://www.pbs.org/wgbh/pages/frontline/gate/. The companion website to the 1998 documentary features a transcript of the film, photographs, an exploration of some of the themes of the 1989 student movement, a timeline, links to speeches and newspaper articles, and book recommendations.

Gay, Kathlyn. *Mao Zedong's China*. Minneapolis: Twenty-First Century Books, 2008. Gay examines the roots of the Communist revolution, Mao's rise to power, life for ordinary people under Mao's dictatorship, and the internal power struggles that led to the Cultural Revolution. Gay wraps up the book with a look at Mao's legacy in modern China.

Shen Tong. *Almost a Revolution*. With Marianne Yen. Boston: Houghton Mifflin, 1990. Shen Tong was a nineteen-year-old student leader in the spring of 1989. Soon after he fled China, he penned his autobiography, from his childhood in Beijing to his role in the student uprising. Marked by humor, insight, and intelligence, Shen's story gives readers an upfront view of the demonstrations from the students' perspective.

"The Tank Man." http://www.pbs.org/wgbh/pages/frontline/tankman/. Visitors to the website can watch the entire 2006 *Frontline* episode about Tiananmen Square and Tank Man. The website also features analysis and interviews with eyewitnesses, journalists, and China experts.

Wong, Jan. *Red China Blues*. New York: Anchor Books, 1996. As a Canadian teenager of Chinese descent, Wong became enamored of Maoism and Communism. This book details her eye-opening journey to China at the height of the Cultural Revolution. Later, as a journalist staying with other foreign reporters in a Beijing hotel, Wong was an eyewitness to the June 4 clearing of Tiananmen Square.

The images in this book are used with the permission of: © David Turnley/CORBIS, p. 4; © Sean Ramsay/The Image Works, pp. 6–7, 99, 104–105; © Jeff Hunter/ Photographer's Choice RF/Getty Images, p. 9; © Hulton Archive/Getty Images, pp. 10 (top), 11; © AFP/Getty Images, pp. 10 (bottom), 15, 123 (bottom); Library of Congress, p. 12 (LC-USZ62-16530); © Laura Westlund/Independent Picture Service, pp. 14, 34; © JACQUET-FRANCILLON/AFP/Getty Images, p. 17; AP Photo, pp. 18, 22, 74–75; © DAJ/Getty Images, pp. 20–21; © Owen Franken/CORBIS, pp. 24–25; AP Photo/Hout-xinhua, p. 27; AP Photo/Kyodo News, p. 29; Keystone/Eyedea/ Everett Collection, p. 30 (left); © NERCIAT/AFP/Getty Images, p. 30 (right); © Digital Vision/Getty Images, pp. 32–33; © IMAGEMORE Co.,Ltd/Getty Images, p. 35 (top); © johnrochaphoto/China/Alamy, p. 35 (bottom); © Bruce Connolly/CORBIS, p. 36; AP Photo/Elise Amendola, p. 40; © Richard Harrington/Hulton Archive/Getty Images, p. 43; © Patrick Riviere/Getty Images, p. 44; AP Photo/Mark Avery, pp. 50–51, 53, 88, 89, 111; © Best View Stock/Alamy, p. 54; © Peter Turnley/CORBIS, pp. 56–57; ©THOMAS CHENG/AFP/Getty Images, p. 67; AP Photo/John Stonham, p. 68; © Forrest Anderson/Time & Life Pictures/Getty Images, p. 71; © Patrick Durand/ CORBIS SYGMA, p. 77; AP Photo/Sadayuki Mikami, pp. 78, 81; © CATHERINE HENRIETTE/AFP/Getty Images, p. 79; AP Photo/Terril Jones, p. 91; AP Photo/Vincent Yu, p. 93; AP Photo/Jeff Widener, File, pp. 94, 109; AP Photo/Jeff Widener, pp. 95, 101; AP Photo/Liu Heung Shing, p. 100; REUTERS/STR New, p. 113; © Stephen Ferry/Liaison/Getty Images, p. 119; © Chris Niedenthal/Time Life Pictures/Getty Images, p. 120; ©Tim Graham/Getty Images, p. 123 (top); © MARK RALSTON/AFP/ Getty Images, p. 124; REUTERS/Andrew Wong, p. 125; © PAUL RICHARDS/AFP/ Getty Images, p. 129; © MIKE CLARKE/AFP/Getty Images, p. 130.

Cover: AP Photo/Jeff Widener, File.

ABOUT THE AUTHOR

Ann Kerns has edited many nonfiction books for young readers and is the author of *Australia in Pictures*, *Romania in Pictures*, *Martha Stewart*, and *Troy*. She enjoys reading, travel, cooking, and music. A native of Illinois, she now lives in Minneapolis, Minnesota.